GOLDEN HART GUIDES

WINDSOR & THE THAMES VALLEY

GOLDEN HART GUIDES

Windsor
& the
Thames Valley

Geoffrey Hindley

SIDGWICK & JACKSON LONDON
in association with Trusthouse Forte

Front cover photo: Windsor Castle
from the Thames
Back cover photo: Hughenden Manor
Frontispiece: St Mary's Church, Amersham

Photographs by the British Tourist
Authority with the exception of the
following: ps. 41, 50, 51, 53 (gracious
permission of HM The Queen); 23, 70
(Pitkin Pictorials); 24 (Christopher Ridley);
32 (British Museum); 36 (Mansell
Collection); 40 (The Beerbohm Estate); 46
(Jeremy Marks/Woodmansterne); 49 (Andy
Williams); 63 (Geoffrey Hindley)

Compiled and designed by Paul Watkins
Editorial associate: Jo Darke
Maps: John Flower

First published in Great Britain 1985
by Sidgwick & Jackson in association
with Trusthouse Forte

ISBN 0-283-99204-2

Photoset by Falcon Graphic Art Ltd,
Wallington, Surrey
Printed and bound in Great Britain
by Hazell Watson and Viney Limited,
Aylesbury, Bucks
for Sidgwick & Jackson Limited,
1 Tavistock Chambers, Bloomsbury Way,
London WC1A 2SG

Contents

Introduction

The Compleat Angler, Marlow

The royal palace of Windsor, the world's largest inhabited castle and one of Europe's chief historical sites, is the natural focus of this book. The valley of the Thames, from Hampton Court Palace in the east to the Goring Gap in the west, runs through the heart of our territory and is its geographical theme. Northward lie the slopes of the Chiltern Hills and the beech groves of South Buckinghamshire. The great houses there, from Cliveden to Hughenden Manor, have provided the rural retreats for two centuries of politicians while, on the north-west fringe of our territory, West Wycombe, with its Hell Fire Caves, recalls the rumours of the notorious orgies of the aristocratic 18th-c. rakes and radicals who grouped themselves into the Hell Fire Club and first convened at Medmenham Abbey on the Thames.

Just a few miles upstream from the Abbey's ruins lie Pangbourne and lovely Mapledurham House, for ever associated with the peaceful idylls of Kenneth Grahame's *The Wind in the Willows*. Along the river we travel through such delightful resorts as Marlow and Boulter's Lock in the company of Jerome K. Jerome's *Three Men in a Boat* to Henley and its world-famous rowing regatta. Westward stands the university of Reading and the beginnings of England's 'silicone valley', for a decade and more a centre of the country's advanced electronic industries.

Northwards again we continue to Amersham and the villages of Penn and Jordans, cradle of the Society of Friends and resting place of the early Quakers, among them William Penn, founder of Pennsylvania. A few minutes away by car, in Chalfont St Giles, stands the cottage where John Milton, a fugitive from the Great Plague of London, completed *Paradise Lost*.

Just over the river from Windsor stands Eton College; down-river a few miles we come to Runnymede, where King John appended his seal to Magna Carta in 1215. A few miles away to the south-west the thrills of Ascot races await. Even the depressing urban sprawl of Slough can boast in its suburbs the village of Stoke Poges, the inspiration of Thomas Gray's *Elegy in a Country Churchyard*.

It is the genius of England that almost every square mile of the country is crammed with history and beauty. Yet few regions even of England are as rich as the one covered by this book. Only a short car journey from Heathrow International Airport, Windsor Castle in the Royal County of Berkshire is a world in itself and the heart of a lovely landscape packed with interest, leisure and sporting opportunities, and with the vibrant echoes of traditions and events that have helped shape the modern world.

The Best of the Region

excluding Windsor Castle (p.20)

A summary of the places of interest in the region, open to the public. The location, with map reference, and description of each place, is shown in the Gazetteer. Names in bold are Gazetteer entries, and those with an *asterisk are considered to be of outstanding interest. (NT) indicates properties owned by the National Trust

Drawing Room, Hughenden Manor

Churches

Those listed here are specially worth a visit, either for the building itself, or for some special feature such as brasses, heraldry, tombs or wall-paintings. Unfortunately, an increasing number of churches are kept locked against vandalism and theft; in most cases, however, a notice on the door or in the porch shows where the key may be borrowed.

* **Amersham** St Mary

  Bisham All Saints'

  Burnham St Peter

  Chalfont St Giles St Giles

  Cookham Holy Trinity

* **Dorney** St James
* **Eton** Eton College Chapel
* **Fingest** St Bartholomew

  Fulmer St James

  Hambleden St Mary

  Henley St Mary

* **Iver** St Peter
* **Langley Marish** St Mary

  Mapledurham St Margaret

* **Penn** Holy Trinity

  Rotherfield Greys St Nicholas

* **Stoke Poges** St Giles

  Taplow Church

  Upton St Lawrence

* **Windsor Castle** St George's Chapel (see p.45)

Historic Buildings

Admission to most historic buildings is between £1-£2.50 (children half-price).

Chalfont St Giles Milton's Cottage (NT)
Feb-Oct, Tue-Sat & Bank Hol Mons 10-1 & 2-6, Sun 2-6; Nov, Sat & Sun only

Cliveden (NT)
House (Hall & Dining Room) closed all 1985. From 1986 Apr-Oct, Sat & Sun 2-6 (last admission 5.30). Grounds Mar-Dec, daily 11-6; Christmas closed

Dorney Dorney Court
Easter-mid Oct, Sun & Bank Hol Mons, Jun-Sep Mon & Tue also, 2-5.30 (last admission 5)

* **Eton** Eton College
Apr-Sep, term time 2-5, holidays 10.30-5 (closed Sat nearest 4 Jun & Sat of Eton Action Week in Sep). College Chapel also open Oct-Apr, daily 2-5

Goring & Streatley Basildon Park
Apr-Oct, Wed-Sat 2-6, Sun & Bank Hol Mons 12-6 (last admission to house 5.30). Closed Good Fri

* **Hampton Court Palace**
May-Sep, Mon-Sat 9.30-6, Sun 11-6; Oct-Apr, Mon-Sat 9.30-5, Sun 2-5, Nov-Feb till 4 (last admission ½hr before closing). Closed 24-26 Dec, 1 Jan & Good Fri
Grounds open daily 7.30-½hr before dusk

Henley-on-Thames The Kenton Theatre
Open for performances only

Hughenden Hughenden Manor (NT)
Mar Sat & Sun, Apr-Oct Wed-Sat, 2-6 or dusk; Sun & Bank Hol Mons from 12 (last admission 5.30)

Jordans Old Meeting House
Wed-Sun 10-6 (Mon 10-1)

Mapledurham Mapledurham House
Easter Sun-Sep, Sat, Sun & Bank Hol Mons, house 2.30-5.30, country park & picnic area 12-7, watermill 12.30-5; winter (all) Sun 2-4

Rotherfield Greys Greys Court (NT)
Apr-Sep, house Mon, Wed & Fri, grounds Mon-Sat, 2-6 (last admission 5.30)

Stonor Park
Apr-Sep, Wed, Thur & Sun; Aug, also Sat, 2-5.30, Bank Hol Mons 11-5.30 (last admission 5)

West Wycombe West Wycombe Park (NT)
Jun Mon-Fri, Jul & Aug Sun-Fri, also Summer Bank Hol Mon, 2-6 (last admission 5.30); also Easter & Spring Bank Hol Suns & Mons (grounds only)

WINDSOR CASTLE see p.45

Parks, Gardens & Wildlife

Admission to the gardens of historic buildings is usually included in a combined ticket for house and garden. (See admission to historic buildings above.) Where the garden can be visited separately this is usually about half the price of the combined ticket. The entrance fee for other gardens open to the public is usually in the range 30-50p (children half-price or less).

* **Cliveden**
House & grounds
See *Historic Buildings*

Chalfont St Giles Chiltern Open Air Museum (Newland Park)
Museum in parkland
See *Museums & Galleries*

Dorney Dorney Court
House & gardens
See *Historic Buildings*

Dorneywood (NT)
Grounds of 20th-c. mansion Aug-Sep, Sat 2.15-6. Admission by written application from the Secretary, Dorneywood Trust, Dorneywood, Bucks

Goring & Streatley Basildon Park
House & park
See *Historic Buildings*

Goring & Streatley Childe Beale
Wildlife Trust
Apr-Sep, Mon, Wed, Thur, Sat &
Sun 10-6

★ **Hampton Court Palace**
Palace & grounds
See *Historic Buildings*

★ **Hughenden** Hughenden Manor
House & garden
See *Historic Buildings*

Mapledurham Mapledurham House
House, country park & working
watermill
See *Historic Buildings*

Rotherfield Greys Greys Court
House & grounds
See *Historic Buildings*

Runnymede Meadows
See *Castles, Ruins, Monuments &*
Ancient Sites

Staines Thorpe Park
Pleasure park
Apr-early Aug, daily 10-6 (from mid-
Jul 10-9)

Stoke Poges Black Park & Langley
Park
Public gardens

Stonor Park
House & deer park
See *Historic Buildings*

West Wycombe Farm & Forest
Trail
Waymarked walk

West Wycombe
West Wycombe Park
House & park
See *Historic Buildings*

Windsor Great Park
(Including The Savill Gardens,
Valley Gardens and Virginia Water)
p.45

Windsor Safari Park & Seaworld
Daily 10-5.30 or dusk (not 25 Dec)

Castles, Ruins, Monuments & Ancient Sites

These sites are accessible at all
reasonable times

Cookham Round Barrows, Cock
Marsh (NT)
Bronze Age/Anglo-Saxon burial
mounds

Gerrards Cross (Bulstrode Park)
Iron Age hill fort

Hurley Monastery
Benedictine monastery ruins

Maidenhead Robin Hood's Arbour
Iron Age earthwork

Reading Abbey
Abbey ruins

Runnymede Meadows (NT)
Thames-side and island site of Magna
Carta Memorial; also John F. Kennedy
& Runnymede Memorials

Slough Salt Hill
Prehistoric tumulus

Stoke Poges Gray's Monument (NT)
Thomas Gray memorial

West Wycombe Mausoleum
Monument
18th-c. monument

WINDSOR CASTLE see p.45

Museums & Galleries

Chalfont St Giles Chiltern Open Air
Museum (Newland Park)
Easter Sun-Oct, Wed, Sun & Bank
Hols 2-6

Chalfont St Giles Milton's Cottage
Museum
See *Historic Buildings*

Cookham Stanley Spencer Gallery
Easter-Oct, daily 10.30-6; Nov-Easter,
Sat, Sun & Bank Hol Mons 11-1 & 2-5

Eton (College) Museum of Eton Life
See *Historic Buildings*

Hampton Court Palace Orangery
Mantegna paintings
See *Historic Buildings*

High Wycombe Wycombe Chair & Local History Museum
Mon, Tue & Thur-Sat 10-1 & 2-5. Closed Bank Hol Mon

Hughenden Hughenden Manor Disraeli Museum
See *Historic Buildings*

Langley Marish Kederminster Library
Open by arrangement. Apply to: The Rev Pierce, The Rectory, St Martin's Road, Langley, Tel (75) 42068; or Mrs Muriel Kemp, 15 Springate Fields, Langley, Tel (75) 42205

Maidenhead Henry Reitlinger Bequest
Apr-Sep, Tue & Thur 10-12.30 & 2.15-4.30, also 1st Sun in month, 2.30-4.30

Reading Cole Museum of Zoology (Reading University)
Mon-Fri 9-5, closed Bank Hols

Reading Museum & Art Gallery
Mon-Fri 10-5.30, Sat 10-5; closed Bank Hol Mons

Reading Museum of English Rural Life (Reading University)
Mon-Fri 9-5, closed Bank Hols

Reading Ure Museum of Greek Archaeology (Reading University)
Mon-Fri 9-5, closed Bank Hols

Staines Thorpe Park Aircraft Exhibition
See *Parks, Gardens & Wildlife*

West Wycombe Caves (Hell Fire Caves)
Apr-Sep, Mon-Sat 1-6, Sun 11-6; Oct-Mar, Sat & Sun 12-4

West Wycombe Motor Museum
Apr-Nov, daily 10-6

Weybridge Brooklands Museum
Opens 1986; enquiries to Weybridge Museum (below)

Weybridge Museum
Mon-Fri, 2-5; Aug & all Sats 10-1 & 2-5

WINDSOR CASTLE see p.45

Windsor Household Cavalry Exhibition
Early May-Aug, Sun-Fri 10-1 & 2-5; Sep-early May, Mon-Fri 10-1 & 2-4. Closed Bank Hols. Last admission ½hr before closing

Windsor Royal Mews Exhibition
Jan-Mar & Nov-Dec, Mon-Sat 10.30-3.15, Apr-Oct 10.30-4.45; also May-Aug Sun 10.30-3 (closed 25 & 26 Dec, New Year & Good Friday)

Windsor Royalty & Empire (Windsor & Eton Central Station exhibition)
Daily 9.30-5.30

Industrial & Rural Heritage

Beaconsfield Bekonscot Model Village
Mar-Oct, daily 10-5

High Wycombe Wycombe Chair & Local History Museum
See *Museums & Galleries*

Jordans Mayflower Barn
Daily 9-5

Lacey Green Smock Windmill
May-Sep, Suns & Bank Hol Mons 3-6

Maidenhead Courage Shire Horse Centre
Mar-Oct, Tue-Sun & Bank Hol Mons 11-5 (last admission 4)

Maidenhead Sounding Arch Viaduct by Brunel

Mapledurham House Watermill
Working watermill & produce shop
See *Historic Buildings*

Marlow Suspension Bridge

Reading Museum of English Rural Life (Reading University)
See *Museums & Galleries*

Rotherfield Greys Greys Court
Tudor donkey wheel & wheel house
See *Historic Buildings*

West Wycombe Farm & Forest Trail
See *Parks, Gardens & Wildlife*

Hotels & Historic Inns

† Non-residential inn
(THF) A Trusthouse Forte Hotel

Amersham Bucks
The Crown Hotel (THF)
High Street
Tel (02403) 21541
The inn's Georgian façade merges well with the other period buildings in Amersham's High Street. The main building, many of the beams and inglenooks and much of the panelling date from Elizabethan times. 16th-c. wall paintings can still be seen in some of the rooms; one in the lounge which incorporates the arms of Elizabeth I is said to commemorate the Queen's visit to the nearby *Shardeloes*.

Ascot Berks
The Berystede Hotel (THF)
Bagshot Road, Sunninghill SL5 9JH
Tel (0990) 23311
Built as a private residence, the hotel is an extravaganza of black-on-white timbering, gables, cupola and towerlets. The 9 acres of landscaped gardens are enclosed by pine groves. Beyond the estate to the S are three golf courses; Ascot racecourse lies to the N.

Dorney Bucks
†*The Pineapple*
Lake End Road SL4 6QS
Tel (06286) 62353
Although the inn is close to the motorway, its surroundings are rural; each of the two 18th-c. cottages has its grazing rights on Dorney Common, five minutes' walk away. Some of the old beams are original, and a warm glow comes from the open fireplaces in the winter. The inn's name commemorates the first pineapple ever grown in England, in the garden of the grand house *Dorney Court* (1668).

Goring Oxon
The Miller of Mansfield
High Street RG8 9AW
Tel (04914) 872829
Standing close to the bridge, the inn is a creeper-covered building of brick and flint. The first landlord here, the miller of Mansfield, gave hospitality to King Henry II – some accounts say Henry III – who had become separated from his hunting party in Sherwood Forest. Unaware of his guest's identity, the miller boasted about the contents of the pie (venison poached from the forest) ending, as the ballad goes,

'. . .*say nothing where'ere thou go,*
We would not for two pence
the King should know'

Grateful for his food and lodging, the King pardoned his host and gave him the land by the Thames on which *The Miller of Mansfield* now stands.

Henley-upon-Thames Oxon
The Angel on the Bridge Inn
Henley-on-Thames RG9 1BH
Tel (04912) 5977
One of *The Angel's* cellars incorporates the arch of an earlier bridge here; the inn's terrace overlooks the river. Situated at the crossing point of main routes NW from London, the 17th-c. three-storeyed building may occupy the site of an ancient hospice, 'The Hermitage'. Like other inns here, *The Angel* serves Brakspear's beer, brewed in the town's 18th-c. riverside brewhouse.

The Red Lion
Thameside RG9 1BH
Tel (04912) 2161
The wisteria-covered inn overlooking the Thames near the bridge is said to have been built originally for workers building St Mary's Church in the 17th c. As Henley's main coaching inn it sheltered many historical figures: among royal names are Charles I, George III and the Prince Regent, who consumed 14 mutton chops at a sitting. Dr Johnson and James Boswell stayed here in 1776, and the Duke of Wellington after the Battle of Waterloo. Today's building dates mainly from the Georgian period.

Hurley Berks
Ye Olde Bell Inn
High Street SL6 5LX
Tel (062882) 4244
The present gabled inn dates from the late 16th c., but was founded as a hospice for the Benedictine Priory of St Mary in the 12th c. During World War II, it was unofficial HQ of General Eisenhower for a while; many mementoes remain from that time.

Maidenhead Berks
Boulters Lock Inn
Boulters Lock SL6 8PE
Tel (0628) 21291
Standing beside the lock, the inn occupies an 18th-c. flour mill and was smartly converted in the 1950s. It has fine river views from its terraces.

Marlow Bucks
The Compleat Angler Hotel (THF)
Marlow Bridge SL7 1RG
Tel (06284) 4444
Once *The Angler's Rest*, the hotel building in its superb position overlooking the weir dates from the 17th c; Izaac Walton, author of the immortal *Compleat Angler* (1653), would have known it as a modest riverside inn.

Reading Berks
The Post House Hotel (THF)
Basingstoke Road RG2 0SL
Tel (0734) 875485
A modern hotel and a well-known landmark for travellers on the M4 between London and Heathrow. The hotel with its swimming pool is also close to Windsor and the Thames; the region's association with the Great Western Railway is reflected in the hotel's Great Western Bar.

Windsor Berks
The Castle Hotel (THF)
High Street SL4 1LJ
Tel (95) 51011
The hotel stands opposite the castle in High Street, a handsome Georgian posting house of four storeys with its name in gilded lettering on the façade. Late in the 18th c. an adjoining house was incorporated, and some of its rooms show good plasterwork decoration of the period. In 1814 the Duke of Wellington, receiving the freedom of the borough, was entertained at *The Castle*.
Wren's Old House Hotel
Thames Street SL4 1PX
Tel (95) 61354
Sir Christopher Wren built *The Old House* in 1676 as his residence while he was comptroller of the works at Windsor Castle. With its terraced gardens, it occupies a pleasant position by the bridge crossing to Eton.

Famous Connections

Many famous – or simply unusual – personalities have been connected with Windsor and the Thames Valley. Details of their association will be found in the Gazetteer entries. Many of the kings and queens listed also have close connections with Windsor Castle (see *A Brief History*, p.20 and *Tour of the Castle*, p.45).

Anne, Queen Penn

Astor, Nancy Cliveden

Astor, Waldorf, 2nd Viscount Cliveden

Astor, William Waldorf, 1st Viscount Cliveden

Blagrave, John Reading

Becket, Thomas à Reading

Boleyn, Anne Hampton Court Palace

Brooke, Rupert Lacey Green

Brunel, Isambard Kingdom Slough, Maidenhead

Buckingham, 2nd Duke of Cliveden

Burke, Edmund Beaconsfield

Campion, St Edmund Stonor Park

Canning, George Cliveden

Charles II Dorney Court

Chesterton, G.K. Beaconsfield

Cook, Captain Chalfont St Giles

Dashwood, Sir Francis (Hell Fire Club) Medmenham, West Wycombe

Disraeli, Benjamin Bradenham, Hughenden

Edward IV Eton

Eisenhower, General Hurley

Franklin, Benjamin West Wycombe

Eliot, T.S. Marlow

Grahame, Kenneth Mapledurham, Pangbourne

Gray, Thomas Burnham Beeches, Stoke Poges, Upton

Henry VI Eton

Henry VIII Hampton Court Palace

Herschel, Sir William Slough, Upton

Hickey, William Beaconsfield

Howard, Catherine Hampton Court Palace

Jeffreys, George (Judge Jeffreys) Gerrards Cross

John, King Runnymede

Kennedy, J.F. Runnymede

Knox, John Amersham

Laud, William (Archbishop of Canterbury) Reading

Lind, Jenny Burnham Beeches

Mendelssohn, Felix Burnham Beeches

Milton, John Chalfont St Giles, Langley Marish

Peacock, Thomas Love Marlow

Penn, William Jordans

Pope, Alexander Mapledurham

Shelley, Mary Marlow

Shelley, Percy Bysshe Marlow

Shepard, E.H. Pangbourne

Spencer, Stanley Cookham

Turner, J.M.W. Maidenhead

Victoria, Queen Slough, Windsor

Waller, Edmund Beaconsfield, Penn (Coleshill)

Wilde, Oscar Reading

Wolsey, Thomas Hampton Court Palace

Wren, Sir Christopher Hampton Court Palace, Windsor

Festivals & Events

Many colourful and notable events take place throughout the region. Race meetings are held all the year round at Windsor and Ascot; polo can be watched in Windsor Great Park most summer weekends. Major events are listed below. For events in **Windsor Castle** see p.45.

April *Molesey* Amateur Regatta (2nd week)

May *Reading* Arts Festival (May-Jun); *Weybridge* Amateur Regatta (Spring Bank Hol); *Windsor* Royal Windsor Horse Show (Home Park)

June *Ascot* Royal Ascot (3rd week); *Henley* Royal Regatta (late Jun-early Jul); *Marlow* Regatta (last week); *Reading* Amateur Regatta (Jun), Arts Festival (May-Jun); *Walton-on-Thames* Walton Regatta

July *Eton* College Founder's Day; *Henley* Royal Regatta (late Jun-early July); *Henley* Town Regatta (last Sat, or 1st in Aug); *Windsor* Championship Dog Show (Home Park); *Staines* Amateur Regatta

August *Henley* Town Regatta (last Sat in Jul, or 1st in Aug); *Maidenhead* Regatta; *Molesey* Amateur Regatta (late Aug); *Staines* Boat Regatta (late Aug); *Stonor Park* Chilterns Craft Show

September *Chalfont St Giles* Show; *Windsor* Festival (Sep-Oct); *Windsor* National Carriage Driving Championships (Smith's Lawn)

October *Windsor* Festival of Music (Sep-Oct)

Swan Upping One of the Thames' most celebrated traditions had its origin in the Middle Ages when swans were a great delicacy of the table. Ownership of the swans was divided between the monarch and two City livery companies, the Dyers and Vintners, and the birds' beaks marked accordingly. In the 3rd week of July swanmasters of the Queen and the livery companies row upriver from London as far as Henley, catching and marking the young swans. At Romney Lock, within sight of Windsor Castle, a Loyal Toast is sworn: much of the marking then takes place on the course of the Royal Regatta, at Henley.

The Thames

The Thames as we know it today is a delightful, disciplined river forming a winding leisure park of close-on 100m through south-east England. But navigation was not always so easy. For centuries the river was liable to flood its banks, with rapids breaking the sometimes sluggish stream as it wended its way between marshy meadows and islands known as 'eyots' or 'aits'. By degrees, the river was brought under control with embankments, weirs and locks to transform it into an ever more important inland waterway. This commercial function was dominant during the 19th century. Today, the locks and weirs chiefly serve cruisers, yachts and pleasure boats of all descriptions which throng the stream throughout the summer and offer the bankside tourist a kaleidoscope of bustling activity and scenic views.

In the heyday of late Victorian and Edwardian England the working life of the river was already being encroached on by holiday makers, chiefly from London. The steam launches of the rich jostled with skiffs and rowing boats along the waterfronts of the pretty riverside towns from Chertsey to Marlow and Henley; Boulter's Lock during those sun-drenched afternoons was abustle with elegant boaters and boisterous horseplay. It was in the 1860s that the flat bottomed 'punt', the maid-of-all-work for the traditional riverman,

was adapted as a pleasure craft. Today most of the Thames-side towns have their punting or rowing regattas, while Henley is home of the world's most famous international regatta. The fisherman will find most classes catered for, while the numerous boatyards offer a full range of hire-craft and pleasure cruises. From the royal palace of Hampton Court to the great castle of Windsor, the river runs like a ribbon through England's history, passing the meadows of Runnymede with its memories of Magna Carta, and the renowned playing fields of Eton. Beyond Windsor the route takes us up to Cookham, home of Stanley Spencer, eccentric and painter extraordinary, and further still to the meadows of Mapledurham House, the inspiration for Toad Hall in Kenneth Grahame's *The Wind in the Willows*.

Between Datchet and Sunbury, a chain of reservoirs serves the needs of the surrounding communities and feeds the supplies of the metropolis on the estuary. Together with the elaborate civil engineering works which have tamed the river itself, they have come to blend into the landscape while constituting a lasting monument to England's industrial and rural heritage.

These important if unobtrusive works require constant maintenance under the direction of the Thames Water Authority and the Thames Conservancy Board, while the River Thames Society, Tel Cobham (0932 26) 7036, is active in extending the amenities of the river. A list of the locks and associated amenities between Hampton Court and Goring follows.

Sport and Recreation

Boat trips There are several companies which run pleasure cruises in the season, or have launches available for charter trips:

Aquadine Enterprises St George and Dragon Boathouse, Wargrave, Berks. Tel (073522) 2485. Cruises available for groups or party hire

D&T Scenics c/o Mapledurham House, near Reading, Berks. Tel (0734) 724123. Regular trips from Caversham Bridge, Reading, to Mapledurham House

French Brothers Runnymede Boathouse, Windsor Road, Old Windsor, Berks. Tel (95) 51900. Regular trips from Runnymede to Hampton Court

Salter Brothers Folly Bridge, Oxford. Tel (0865) 243421. Variety of trips offered between Reading and Henley and from Windsor upstream to Maidenhead and Marlow, and downstream to Runnymede and Staines. Details of sailing times from Reading (0734) 52388 and Windsor (95) 65832

Windsor Boats The Promenade, Windsor & Mill Lane, Windsor, Berks. Tel (95) 62933. 33 min return trips to Boveney Lock, with views of Windsor Castle and Eton College, and 2hr return trips, with bar and refreshments, through Boveney Lock to Monkey Island

Boating on the Thames Anyone planning a full boating holiday will find many excellent specialist publications; a wealth of basic information is provided by *Stanfords Map of the River Thames from Lechlade to Richmond*, available from bookshops. An excellent guide published by the Thames & Chilterns Tourist Board in conjunction with the Thames Hire Cruiser Association and Thames Water is *The Thames: Royal River*, which lists the boatyards which are members of the Association and offers information on cruising holidays. The guide is obtainable from the Tourist Board at the address on p.19 (send large s.a.e.).

The following is a list of the locks between Hampton Court and Goring, with general points of interest and boatyards where boat hire is possible.

HAMPTON COURT

River miles from Romney Lock (Windsor)	Lock	Boatyards in vicinity
18	**Molesey** River's second longest lock; swimming pool and pleasure gardens nearby. Rollers for small boats	B.J.A. Martin, Constable's Boathouse 01-941 4858
15	**Sunbury**	Turks of Sunbury (09327) 82028 G. Wilson & Sons (09327) 82067
13	**Shepperton**	D.B.H. Marine (0932) 228019/42379
10	**Chertsey** Good pike fishing	Chertsey Meads Marine (09328) 64699 W. Bates & Son (09328) 62255/6
9	**Penton Hook**	Penton Hire Cruisers (09328) 64122
6	**Bell Weir** Good fly fishing; rollers for small boats	J. Tims & Son (81) 52093 Biffins Boatyard (81) 52408
3	**Old Windsor**	Crevalds Services (95) 60393
0	**Romney** Nearest lock to Windsor, scene of annual swan upping ceremony. Backwater by the long ait popular for boating parties	John Hicks Boatyard (75) 43930 Tom Jones (Boatbuilders) (95) 60699
3	**Boveney** Rollers for small boats; Monkey Island Hotel upstream	

6	**Bray** Monkey Island Hotel downstream	
8	**Boulters** Favourite river resort near Maidenhead	Bert Bushnell (0628) 24061 Bray Boats (0628) 37880
10	**Cookham** Beautiful backwater of Odney Pool nearby; bathing and children's pool	Turks Boatyard (06285) 20110 Andrews Boathouses (06285) 22314 Bourne End Marina (06285) 22813/4
14	**Marlow** Good coarse fishing downstream; National Scout Boating Activity Centre	
16	**Temple** Rollers for small boats	
17	**Hurley**	Peter Freebody's (062882) 4382
20	**Hambleden** Footpath and footbridges across dramatic weirs with fine mill at Mill End (see also *Walk 3*, p.18)	Hambleden Mill Boatyard (049166) 316
23	**Marsh** Long and picturesque wooden bridge and weir; nearest lock to Henley	Hobbs & Sons 0491 572035 Hooper's of Henley 0491 576867
26	**Shiplake**	Swancraft, Henley (073522) 2577
29	**Sonning** Well-tended gardens	
32	**Caversham** (Reading) Swimming baths near lock	Caversham Boat Services (0734) 54323
36	**Mapledurham** The oldest mill on the river nearby; Mapledurham House	
38	**Whitchurch** Notable scenery; footbridge from Swan Inn at Pangbourne; triple weir and numerous islands	
42	**GORING**	

Fishing Below Staines, fishing in the Thames is free; above that point rod licences are required and, with weir permits, may be had on application to Thames Water Authority, Reading, Tel (0734) 593300. The principal weirs are at Bray, Boveney, Bell, Goring, Marsh, Molesey, Old Windsor, Romney, Shepperton, Shiplake and Sunbury

Day tickets for coarse fishing near Marlow are available from Westhorpe Farm, Marlow, and the close season for coarse fishing is from March 15 to June 15. Fishing from boats along most reaches also requires a permit from the association or club covering the relevant stretch of river. Boating and fishing are increasing in popularity on the Thames, and it pays to be on the scene early in the day during the summer and autumn.

Golf The following golf clubs in the region admit non-members on advance application and payment of the standard green fees:
Ascot; Burnham Beeches; Calcot (Reading); Caversham & S. Oxon (Emmer Green); Datchet (Windsor); Denham (Uxbridge); Farnham Common (Burnham Beeches); Goring & Streatley; Henley; Hurley; Knotty Green (Beaconsfield); Maidenhead; Stoke Poges; Sunningdale; Temple (Hurley); Wentworth (Ascot).

Walks

The public footpaths in this area are better sign-posted than perhaps anywhere else in England. There is a wide variety of beautiful walks in the region, from the beechwoods of Buckinghamshire to the banks of the Thames. For the enthusiast walker the following publications are recommended: *Chilterns Walks for Motorists: Southern Area* by Nicholas Moon (1979); *Discovering Walks in the Chilterns* by Ron Pigram (1982); *Chiltern Round Walks* by V.B. Burden (1974). However, the tourist in this region should not forget the marvellous walks through the grounds of Cliveden House, Windsor Great Park and the Savill Gardens, in addition to the circular routes detailed below.

Walk 1 *West Wycombe Farm and Forest Trail*

Established by the Chiltern Society in 1973, the Trail is a circuit of rough open grassland and cultivated fields with the mid-17th-c., half-timbered Chorley Farm house as a special attraction. The walk starts below St Lawrence's Church near the A40, and is clearly marked with white arrows and blue code numbers. Stout walking shoes are recommended, and you should be prepared for some steepish climbs/3½m

Walk 2 *Burnham Beeches*

Purchased by the Corporation of the City of London in the 1870s, these beautiful woodlands are still unspoiled and an invitation to the rambler. There is car parking at East Burnham Common. From the car park head N across the road and follow the woodland path that leads down to a hollow with a culvert over a stream. Continue straight on until the path converges with the road, and follow the road through the village of Egypt (perhaps so-called because once a site of gypsy settlement). On the outskirts of the village a concrete drive (footpath) leads off to the left between buildings. The path leads ¾m through woods to a stile which you cross. Keeping to the hedge you come to a road at an elbow bend; continue along it straight ahead. Fork left shortly for the village of Littleworth Common. Through the village, turn left at the junction by the pub and follow the road to a left turn (straight on leads to Dorneywood in ¾m).

Taking the turn, continue past a cross-roads, up Pumpkin Hill and past a three-ways. A little further on a forest road signed Burnham Beeches leads left into the woods, past an ancient earthwork and back to East Burnham Common car park/4½m

Walk 3 *Henley to Hambleden Lock and Mill End*

Starting from Henley Bridge on the right bank, follow the towpath past the Leander Club and on to Hambleden Lock, a distance of about 2m. From the lock a long footbridge carries the path over the weirs to Hambleden Mill and boatyard, and a minor road leads N from the A4155 through Mill End to the village of Hambleden. From the mill you may either return along the way you have come or join the A4155. Turning left you follow the road for about ¾m, passing the gates of the Administrative Staff College on your left. Shortly after this you will find a footpath signposted on your left which leads back across fields to join the towpath opposite Temple Island. Skirting Fawley Meadows for a time, you make your way along Henley Reach to Henley/6m

Walk 4 *Fingest to Turville*

Park by Fingest Church. After visiting the church turn right at the T junction (facing *The Chequers Inn*) and right again at the stile by the small green marked with a public footpath sign. Follow along to the wood, turning left along its edge to a minor road: crossing the road and a stile rejoin the footpath and continue along the edge of a copse to a further stile which is crossed into a field. Downhill across the field a stile leads into the village of Turville. Visit the church and *The Bull and Butcher Inn*. Next return to the stile for the path up Turville Hill to the old mill at the top. Beyond, you turn right along the road for some 30 yds before turning left into the woods. Follow the main path downhill to a charming country lane at a long gate. Here turn right to return to Fingest. A short but delightful stroll in beautiful Chilterns countryside with visits to characteristic village churches and pubs/1½m

Walk 5 *Greys Court and Rotherfield Greys*

Bearing half left at the tollgate to the E of the house and following the fence, you join the waymarked route and cross four stiles to a track which leads past a pond on the right and farm buildings on the left. At the minor road at the end of the track turn right towards the village of Broadplat, then left at the junction for a short distance to a waymarked path on the right into Lambridge Wood. After ½m, keeping straight through the wood, turn right where paths cross (crossed arrows on tree) and continue downhill slightly for ¼m looking out for a stile on the right. Cross this and over undulating field to further stile. A second stile is then crossed to reach the stile at the main road. Turning right, cross the road to the waymarked route to the left (New Farm). This starts as a concrete road and then becomes a track, bearing right. A footpath leads left off this and follows the edge of a field to a stile. Cross this, taking another path to the right, and shortly on the left the fence is crossed to follow another path over a hill to the village of Rotherfield Greys. Here, after a drink perhaps in *The Maltster's Arms*, walk back along the road to Greys Court/3m

Walk 6 *Cookham river bank and Winter Hill*

From the car park to the W of the village (Cookham Moor) take the public footpath from the stile at the corner of the moor. This follows the right side of a field to a second stile which is crossed to join a gravel path to the river bank. Turn left and follow the towpath around the river bend passing under a railway bridge and on past a line of bungalows. At the white Ferry Cottage further on, turn left onto a concrete path and follow for 200 yds. At the right bend in this path a dirt track leads across a field to the hillside

over a stile. Follow the path to the right along the flank of the hill. Cross a stile at the top to join a minor road and double back left. At the second bend, leave the road by the stile and footpath to right. Follow the electricity posts and then over further stile to follow path between fenced paddocks. Over the stile at the end, cross the lane to a hedged field. Entering the field by a stile, bear right across it to join minor road and follow downhill and over railway line to Cookham/4½m

Motoring Tours

The noteworthy sights in our area are so numerous and so comparatively accessible from Windsor that the reader will no doubt prefer to make a personal selection of routes. However, two suggestions may be made: one for a day trip starting from London, the other for an outing from Windsor itself.

Tour 1 *London–Windsor–Eton–Cliveden*
Leave London on M4 motorway; take Exit 6 for Windsor and Eton; from Windsor take B3026 and then B476 for Cliveden; after Cliveden continue along B476, then A4094 to Exit 3 on M40, and so return to London. An early start from London will leave time to see Eton College, Windsor Castle and its environs, and the grand house and grounds at Cliveden, while the cross-country route offers delightful views of the English countryside.

Tour 2 *Windsor and the Thames*
From Windsor take A308 to Maidenhead, then on to A423 for Henley; here follow signs to Rotherfield Greys. Return to Henley, then take A4155 to Marlow and Bourne End and A4094 S to Cookham; cross A4 to Bray by B3028; follow road by river to A308, and so back to Windsor

Further Information Leaflets and information on leisure activities, accommodation, etc. in the region are available from the Thames & Chilterns Tourist Board, 8 Market Place, Abingdon Oxfordshire OX14 3UD. Tel (0235) 22711.

Windsor Castle

A Brief History

The chief residence of the English royal house and the largest inhabited castle in the world, Windsor Castle stands on a low hill on the south bank of the Thames with the shops and houses of the town of Windsor coming up to the gates. Away to the south stretches Windsor Great Park, reached from the castle by the Long Walk; to the east, Home Park runs down to the river. The calm and elegant beauty of the setting, and the markedly residential character of the Castle today, tend to obscure the natural strength of the site so that, in spite of the mighty curtain wall and its towers, the visitor may be tempted to forget the original purpose of the place and to think only of the chivalry and pomp of its later history. And yet, apart from the Tower of London, this was the main stronghold of the first Norman kings of England.

The first castle on the site was built by William the Conqueror, probably about 1070, as part of his programme of consolidation of the victory at Hastings some four years

before. The castles of the invaders were soon springing up in every English shire; Windsor was built to defend the approach to the capital down the Thames Valley. The site was protected to the north by the river and by the sharp slope of its hill, and was little more than a good day's march from London.

King William's castle was of the motte and bailey type, the natural strength of the site being reinforced by the great earth mound or 'motte' above which rose a wooden tower. Most of the Normans' immediate post-conquest castles were of this type, since it was quick and simple to erect and offered adequate security against the disorganized and demoralized local opposition which was all the conquerors anticipated. Today, despite centuries of development, the fortress-palace still centres on the original primitive mound, though the Round Tower which now surmounts it is characterized by Georgian Gothick of the early 19th century.

The Norman Kings The original wooden tower and its motte were protected by three outer wards, or courtyards, divided from one another by ditch and rampart as added obstacles to an attacker. There were to be no major changes at Windsor for the next 80 years, nor was the military history of the place particularly memorable. The desultory, if vicious campaigns between King Stephen and Matilda produced anarchy in England but largely passed Windsor by. Then, in 1154, Matilda's son ascended the throne as King Henry II. Henry's most pressing problem was to restore royal authority against powerful barons in scores of unauthorized or 'adulterine' castles. Henry ordered the destruction of these strongholds and strengthened the royal seats of power. During his reign (1154-89), the wooden fortifications at Windsor were replaced by a stone tower and stone walls. Of these, only the lower masonry courses of the tower, providing the basis for the Round Tower, survive. The apartments built for Henry in the Upper and Lower Wards have long since disappeared.

Perhaps the greatest of all England's kings, Henry brought justice and peace to the troubled kingdom, but his firm rule provoked growing discontent among the barons, which grew into full-scale rebellion when his younger son John (1199-1216) continued the rigorous regime of his father without the ability to retain the loyalty of the great men. It was at this time that Windsor withstood the only two sieges of its history. The first was in 1193 when John took and garrisoned the place during the absence of his brother Richard I on crusade, and the second in 1215 when John's castellan was besieged – unsuccessfully – by the rebellious barons.

Like his father, Henry III was faced with civil war, and the next stage of the fortifications at Windsor went up during his reign (1216-72). The Salisbury, Garter and Curfew Towers of the southwest wall are the principal structures surviving from this period. The conical roof on Curfew Tower was added in the 1860s, though possibly all three were originally covered in this way. Henry also built a Chapel to St Edward the Confessor, later demolished, and, with other work, completed the transformation of Windsor into a palace – late in the 13th century a chronicler described it as the most magnificent in Europe. It thronged with courtiers; in the 1240s the king had regulated the number of horses stabled within the walls because the smell was thought to be endangering the health of his young son, Prince Edward.

Medieval chivalry The next great period of building was under King Edward III, born at Windsor, (1327-77), during whose reign the Castle was enriched with a series of royal apartments and became the centre of the king's Order of the Garter, the first of the European orders of chivalry. The works at Windsor during the 1350s were supervised by William of Wykeham; although of peasant birth, he was appointed surveyor of the king's works in 1356 and later rose to become Bishop of Winchester and a principal royal adviser. At

The pride of English chivalry was gloriously crowned in the year 1346 when the royal army defeated the French at the Battle of Crecy and the northern barons defeated the Scots, bringing the Scottish King David II in triumph as prisoner to Windsor. Ten years later Poitiers marked another dazzling victory over the French and this time their king, John II, was brought captive to England.

Founding of the Garter The king had announced his intention to 'begin a Round Table in the same manner and conditions as the Lord Arthur, formerly King of England, appointed it,' in 1344. The original intention was for a company of some 300 knights who, by the symbolism of the Round Table, were accounted all equal in status within the Order. However, the Garter as we know it today, a select body of 25 and the sovereign, seems to have been inaugurated at jousts held in Windsor in the spring of 1348 and the 'garter' itself may have been no more than the badge worn by two teams of twelve knights, one led by the king, the other by the Black Prince. The well known legend as to its origin dates from about a century later. The early statutes of the Order have been lost, and for centuries scholars and antiquaries have sought to discredit the romantic story, but inconclusively. At a ball in Windsor, it was said, the king was dancing with Joanne, Countess of Salisbury when her garter slipped off. Edward gallantly retrieved it. Teased by his courtiers he responded sharply with the words '*Honi soit qui mal y pense* 'shame to him who thinks evil of

The Norman Gate

Windsor, Wykeham began a long association with the mason William of Wynford who collaborated not only on the royal apartments for Edward III but also on Wykeham's foundations at Winchester College and New College, Oxford.

From all their work at Windsor, only the so-called Norman Gateway and their reconstruction of Henry III's Winchester Tower survive. The dazzling new stone of the royal improvements would have provided a fitting setting for the pomp and splendours of Windsor under the tall and warlike King Edward III. The foundation of the Order of the Garter in the mid 1340s won the admiration of royal Europe and it was soon to be imitated by other monarchs. It was all part of the nostalgic romanticism of the late Middle Ages based on the cult of the Arthurian romances.

this.' As the ribaldry continued, the king added that in a short time they would 'see the garter advanced to so high honour as to account themselves happy to wear it.'

Among the 25 founder knights were many young bloods – some of them, no doubt, the champions of those 1348 joustings and not as yet renowned on the battlefield. The Order soon grew to something greater. The oldest of the surviving choir-stall heraldic plates now in St George's Chapel is that of Lord Basset of Drayton, who distinguished himself under the Black Prince on the field of Poitiers. By the end of the century foreign noblemen and even kings had been honoured to be chosen as members.

In founding the Order King Edward was adapting the games of chivalry to his own ends. The code of knightly honour was an effective instrument for blunting the edge of aristocratic ambition. While powerful barons were bound by an oath of honour to their sovereign, the threat of rebellion might be lessened and the bonds of chivalry might even be thought to strengthen ties of alliance with foreign lords. St George, to become the patron saint of England in the next century was made the patron of the order, and Edward III made over Henry III's Chapel of St Edward, the old patron of England, to be the Chapel of the Order.

Ruins and new glories Edward was succeeded in 1377 by his grandson Richard II. The luxury of the brilliant court became a byword, but the internal peace of the kingdom broke down in aristocratic revolts which finally de-

Edward IV, St George's Chapel window

posed Richard. As if to symbolize the crumbling of the state, the Chapel of St George (formerly of St Edward) was ruinous and 'on the point of falling to the ground.' The repairs were put in the charge of Geoffrey Chaucer, whose poetry had delighted the court for a generation but whose income derived from his post as Clerk of the Works in the Palace of Westminster. At the height of King Richard's power no fewer than 10,000 meals a day were served to the court at Windsor and its hangers-on. The Castle's next period of glory came with the reign of King Edward IV (1460-83).

Handsome, over 6ft tall and renowned as a debonair womanizer,

Edward delighted in lavish entertaining in the intervals between the business of government, at which he was outstandingly adept. He and his courtiers were to be seen gliding down the Thames in gilded barges or jousting, banners flying, beneath the walls of the castle. Summer night banquets were followed by dancing and dalliance by moon and torchlight; before dawn the court was on the move 'to be beforehand of the sun in their pursuit of royal disports.' Pleasure-loving, the king also hated inefficiency and needless waste; during the reign *The Black Book of the Household* was issued which prescribed in meticulous detail the rights and duties of the hundreds of household servants who attended upon the king at Windsor and his other palaces. Edward also concerned himself with the Order of the Garter. The old chapel was once again verging on ruin so the king had it demolished and ordered the start on a new building (1478); St George's Chapel, as we know it today, was completed some 40 years later, in the reign of Henry VIII.

The Tudor monarchy Under Henry VIII, Windsor was the scene of festivities which outshone anything that had gone before. Yet perhaps nothing matched the cortège which brought the dead king's body from Westminster to Windsor in the winter of 1547. The roads along the whole length of the route were specially swept and in many places widened. The coffin was borne upon a carriage drawn by eight horses, caparisoned in black and each bearing a page carrying the royal banner. As was the custom, the coffin was surmounted by an effigy of the dead king, but no such effigy had ever been so encrusted with precious stones as that of Henry. In all, the cortège stretched more than 4 miles, and as it drew in sight of the great fortress-palace the choir of the Chapel Royal began to sing solemn litanies of welcome.

The ageing Henry had become so grossly overweight that special pulleys and machines had had to be installed to move him from one floor of his palace to another. But in his youth he had been handsome, athletic and precociously learned. The Renaissance scholar Erasmus described Windsor in the early days of the reign, for all its extravagant gaiety, as the 'home of the Muses.'

Henry's son Edward VI was probably the most talented of all the Tudors. But he was an austere and unhappy boy, who found Windsor, without galleries or gardens for walks, a prison. He came to the throne aged nine and died foul and disfigured, no doubt of syphilis inherited from his father, two months before his 16th birthday. As befitted the unlovely Puritanism of his religious convictions, Edward presided over the destruction of many of the glories of England's medieval churches, and also passed statutes condemning the Garter for 'despicable ceremonies of a Papist origin.'

In the sad reign of his eldest sister Mary I the court was a subdued place and her husband, the Spanish King Philip II, returned to his own kingdom as soon as he decently could after his installation as a Knight of the Garter at Windsor.

When Mary died in 1558 the dark legacy of Henry VIII's brutal and cataclysmic masque of marriage and religion reached its final curtain. Like her sister, Elizabeth had suffered the indignity of bastardization in the course of her father's desperate search for a wife who would give him a male heir. Once her life had seemed at hazard in the interests of her sister's safety on the throne. She had spent an anxious girlhood in retirement and semi-arrest, partly in Windsor where, according to her tutor Roger Ascham, she read more Greek in a day than some prebendaries of the chapel read in a week. As her reign advanced to its glorious zenith the ancient palace returned to days of brilliance and gaiety. The royal apartments were fitted out with fine bathrooms; the sound of the Queen's virginals could be heard; and many a delightful masque was performed within the walls. According to tradition it was at Elizabeth's request that Shakespeare wrote *The Merry Wives of Windsor* to show Sir John Falstaff in love. The chief addition to the structure was a fine terrace, beneath the Queen's apartments on the north side of the Upper Ward, where she could take her walks.

Stuarts and Civil War In 1603 the fading splendours of Gloriana were succeeded by the buffooneries of James I. Learned without wisdom, stubborn without strength, lascivious by inclination and uncouth in appearance, he slobbered with maudlin affection on the handsome young men of his court and took a delight in seeing the ladies debase themselves in suggestive masques. James's consuming passion was hunting. It was the traditional sport of kings, and the parks of Windsor had provided many of his predecessors with more than ample game. Teeming with wildlife, they also provided the burghers of the little town of Windsor with rough shooting. There was enough for all, but James, obsessed with his royal rights and greedy of his pleasures, revived ancient lapsed forest laws to stop the townsmen's sport.

Nothing could have been a greater contrast to the vulgarity of the court of King James than the rigorous formality of the order introduced by his virtuous and sensitive son, Charles I. As convinced of the divine right of his office as had been his father, Charles was the only monarch in Europe, at a time when kings were not noticeably egalitarian, who required that he be served on bended knee. Yet for all its protocol, the court of Charles I was also reckoned by the Venetian ambassador to be the most sumptuous and cheerful in the world. The king's taste as an art connoisseur was justly renowned, but his sensitivity to the needs and hopes of his subjects was slight, and his royal hauteur, coupled with a deviousness in politics which he mistook for statecraft, brought him to a confrontation with Parliament which led to Civil War, and his own death.

At the outbreak of the war the town of Windsor opened its gates to the Parliamentary forces, and after a mere seven hours of bombardment from emplacements in the grounds of Eton College, Royalist artillery under the command of Prince Rupert of the Rhine abandoned the attempt to reduce the garrison in the Castle.

The Parliamentary commander received orders to guard the chapel at Windsor against any Puritan excesses by his troops and to preserve the records of the Order of the Garter from 'defacing'. Despite Royalist slanders to the contrary, he discharged his orders faithfully, though much of the church plate was sold to raise funds for the army, just as the plate of the Oxford college chapels was melted down on the orders of Charles to mint coin for his troops.

With the Civil War won and the king a prisoner, it was at Windsor that the General Officers of the Army met on November 11, 1647 to decide the royal fate. Oliver Cromwell was a principal figure in the discussions which ended with the resolution to prosecute the king for his life. A few weeks later the commanders held a day-long fast of earnest prayer before confirming their decision. The following year, Christmas Day 1648, Charles rode once more into his Castle of Windsor, though this time under armed escort as preparations for his trial went forward in London. He was treated with respect – for the first four days, indeed, his meals were served to the sound of trumpets and he was waited on at table on bended knee. When these rather incongruous privileges were withdrawn the king decided to dine alone rather than 'to diminish his dignity'.

After the king's trial and execution Parliament ordained that he might be buried at Windsor and allowed £500 for the expenses of the funeral. The Royalists did not show the same magnanimity. After his restoration in 1660, King Charles II ordered that Oliver Cromwell's body be disinterred, beheaded and the remains hung on a public gibbet.

17th-century Knight of the Garter

The Merry Monarch The court of Charles II was also in contrast to what had gone before. He came to love Windsor, where he could swim, scull and play tennis in the new courts he built there and where, also, the wives and daughters of the townsmen could be discreetly ushered into the royal bed-chamber, to which only the king and his private servant, William Chiffinch, had the key. In the time of Mary Tudor, the queen often went about the poor of the town incognito, dressed like her waiting women; under the Restoration, the ladies of the court frolicked in the streets, masked and disguised as

Windsor Castle: 17th-century engraving by Wenceslaus Hollar

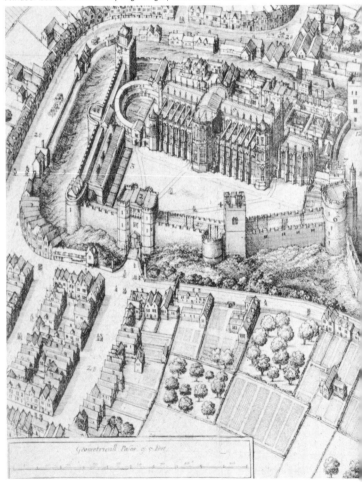

orange girls, entering uninvited the houses of the citizens to dance there. The king's Catholic mistress, the Duchess of Portland, had rooms at the Castle. Nell Gwynne, the king's Protestant whore as she called herself, was accommodated in the town at Burford House, which her son by the king was to inherit. It was all rather different from the stuffy etiquette maintained by Louis XIV at Versailles. Charles did not discount the importance of protocol but he could be relaxed about it. When the pious Quaker, William Penn, was presented to the king at Windsor he kept his hat

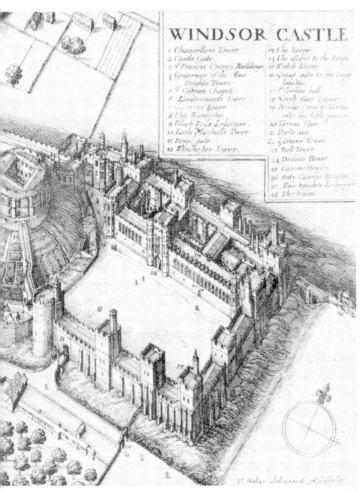

WINDSOR CASTLE

1 Chancellors Tower
2 Castle Gate
3 St Francis Crmes Buildings
4 Governor of the Alms Knights Tower
5 St Georges Chapell
6 Lieutenants Tower
7 Gunners Tower
8 The Wardrobe
9 Black Rods Lodgings
10 Earle Marshalls Tower
11 Pangs gate
12 Winchester Tower

13 The Keepe
14 The ascent to the Keepe
15 Watch Tower
16 Great gate to the Pangs lodgings
17 St Georges hall
18 North East Tower
19 Bridge from ye Terras into the little parter
20 Terras Gate
21 Parke gate
22 Garters Tower
23 Bell Tower
24 Deanes House
25 Canons Houfes
26 Petty Canons Houfes
27 Alms knights Lodgings
28 The Towne

W. Hollar delineavit et sculpsit

29

on, as his principles required. The king said nothing, merely removed his own. 'Friend Charles,' asked Penn, 'why dost thou not keep on thy hat?' ''Tis the custom in this place,' replied the king, 'for only one person to remain covered at a time.'

Prince Rupert of the Rhine, the most dashing commander for the Royalist cause during the Civil War, was appointed governor of the Castle. Prematurely grey with his exertions in the war, he continued his vigorous life, hunting in the parks, experimenting with the new technique of engraving, known as mezzotint, which he had invented, setting the garrison to rights and restoring the structure. During the Commonwealth, Parliament had debated a bill to sell the place but threw it out on learning that Windsor would not fetch more than £2,700. The estate had been kept intact, but the buildings had not been maintained, and over the decade squatters had been allowed to encroach.

Charles authorized large new works under the direction of the architect Hugh May. He also set about reviving the former glories of the Garter ceremonies in what Samuel Pepys considered the 'most romantique castle in the world.' At its banquets held in St George's Hall the king sat in state alone at a high table on the dais. The 25 knights, with high hats adorned with rich plumes and dressed in elaborate new robes designed by the king himself, had their places down a long table backed by a beautiful arras. Beneath the high windows on the opposite wall stood 25 small serving tables from which the knights'

servants served their masters, making their way across the hall between the 12 officers of the College of Arms, who stood in double file with Garter King of Arms at their head facing the high table.

Georgian neglect Charles died a popular king; his brother James II who followed never knew, nor wanted, the gift of popularity. A Catholic, he devoted his short reign to an attempt to restore the old religion and, at least in the first instance, freedom of religion to all his subjects. It may be doubted whether James's toleration would have long outlasted the establishment of Catholicism but even the thought of toleration was too out of tune with the sentiments of his subjects to be given a chance, and he was forced to flee the country.

Neither James, nor his successor, the Dutch king William III, spent much time here. But Queen Anne loved Windsor; before her accession she had spent much time at Burford House and then a house on Castle Hill. As queen, she spent her happiest times here. Her passion for hunting matched that of any previous monarch and when glandular trouble and dropsy made her too fat to ride, she followed the hounds through the forests and parks of Windsor in a one-seat light chariot with immensely high wheels which carried her above the bushy undergrowth, and which she drove herself.

In the last year of her life, Queen Anne became so grotesquely fat that a trap door was made in the floor of her bedroom so that, like Henry VIII, she could be lowered and raised by winch and

St George's Hall: 17th-century engraving by Wenceslaus Hollar

pulley. She died, at last, on August 1, 1714. George, Elector of Hanover, who succeeded her as George I, had no interest in Windsor and for the next 60 years the Castle lay neglected.

Squatters of high and low estate moved into rooms and apartments, some asserting claims on the royal family, others simply settling in. The ditch, which since medieval times had surrounded the Castle, the terraces and the courtyards became playgrounds for the boys of the town. The deserted courts of the Upper Quadrangle echoed to their shouts on moonlit evenings. Hucksters set up their stalls inside the gates; sight-seers, beggars, oyster sellers, orange girls and pedlars wandered at will through the precincts. The buildings fell into decay, and the structure was weakened as the new occupants knocked through walls to open up their rooms or link adjacent apartments with new doorways.

'Mad' King George This sorry state of affairs began to mend in the 1770s when King George III established a residence at Windsor. Rather than disturb the arrangements at the Castle the king, with characteristic generosity, ordered Queen Anne's house almost entirely rebuilt. The king became more and more enchanted with the place. Ill-at-ease in the capital, where his gauche behaviour concealed his fundamental good nature and earned him the contempt of his courtiers, he could relax here in the bosom of his family and play the part of the country squire.

Comfortable though it may have been for the king, the domestic life of the court at Queen's Lodge was excruciatingly dull for everyone else. Daily prayers were held in St George's Chapel and attendance was obligatory. Modestly economical in his lifestyle, the king refused to allow heating in the chapel

The Prince Regent welcoming Lady Conyngham to his 'lonely cot' – Royal Lodge, Windsor

even in the depth of winter. Contemporary court memoirs record the shivering misery of ministers and courtiers, and the king's alarming tendency to keep the dilatory up to their devotions by calling out the place in the prayer book. Most evenings the royal family took their stroll on the castle terrace to the sound of a band.

The king was a familiar figure in the town, dropping in on shopkeepers and tradesmen to examine their wares or advise them on how to vote at election times. One day he came across a copy of Tom Paine's *Rights of Man* in a Windsor bookshop; years later the bookseller's son recalled that the king studied this radical tract for half an hour before returning it to its place and leaving the shop with his customary good-natured greeting to the shopkeeper.

Ten years after taking up his residence in Windsor, King George succumbed to his first attack of madness. Modern research has shown that its cause lay not in mental disorder but in the pain and change in body chemistry brought on by an extremely rare disease, porphyria. But to the medical science of the time the symptoms of the king's wildly erratic behaviour and nervousness – on one occasion he babbled almost incoherently for 16 hours on end – were those of lunacy. He was subjected to treatment both cruel and humiliating, which only made things worse until new doctors took over. They insisted that he leave Windsor for Kew. The king could only be induced to do so when the queen, collaborating with the doctors, secretly left. By March 1789 the new treatment had calmed the king's nerves sufficiently for him to return to Windsor where he was greeted by cheering crowds. An immense public banquet was held to celebrate his return.

To his English subjects George III sometimes seemed stupid – to his American subjects, tyrannical. Yet Benjamin Franklin had said of him that he was the best king any nation was ever blessed with and years after the United States had won their independence the king received their envoy, John Adams, in friendship. In the 1790s he finally made the move into the Castle when staying at Windsor. Now in his sixties, 'Farmer George', as he was affectionately known by the common people, was at his happiest strolling in the castle parks and farms, dressed in the special uniform which he himself had designed for the Windsor militia which he had raised and of which he had appointed himself commander. But the pressures of state and his frequently acrimonious relations with ministers often depressed him and once, according to the Prince of Wales, he considered abdicating and retiring to America itself.

The king's 'madness' had terrified Queen Charlotte, and the domestic bliss which had been theirs faded. The queen spent more and more of her time in her 'little paradise', the estate of Frogmore in the Park where she laid out the beautiful gardens. The king spent most of his days in a dark room overlooking the North Terrace where he had once delighted to walk. He died at Windsor on the evening of January 29, 1820.

King Prinny When he came to the throne George IV had already built up a fund of public ill-will through his extravagance, which had to be met by Parliament. His pleasure pavilion at Brighton had cost thousands – the works which he authorized at Windsor to designs by Jeffrey Wyatville were to rise from an estimated £125,000 to more than £800,000. When they were complete the Castle presented much the appearance that it does today. His reign opened with the scandalous failure of his attempt to divorce his wife, to general public delight and derision, and he retired to Windsor to lick his wounds.

Taking over a ranger's cottage in the ground he had it enlarged and remodelled in picturesque style by John Nash. This 'Cottage Orné' (the Royal Lodge) became the king's principal retreat while at Windsor. For most of the king's reign it was the centre of the kind of scandal which had dogged the ageing monarch for most of his life. In the early months, George entertained the representatives of Europe's most reactionary governments here while his own ministers pursued a liberal policy; but his liaison with Lady Conyngham provided much juicy themes for court gossips. The 'young lovers' were both over fifty and both horribly overweight. The king's infatuation in public was ludicrous and the favours showered upon Lady Conyngham, her husband and her relations, who descended in force, outrageous. While courtiers took umbrage the cartoonists had a field day.

The king banned Home Park to the people of Windsor. But the

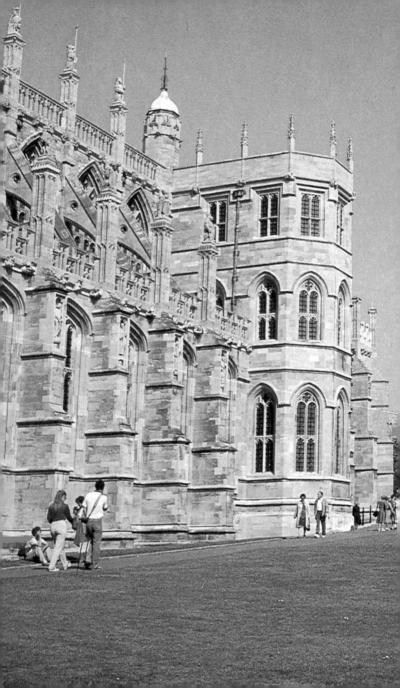

Windsor Great Park in Victorian times

more he sought seclusion the more unpopular he became. Self-indulgent and often petulant, the king was fundamentally good-natured, generous to his friends and kindly to children. Queen Victoria was to recall happy girlhood days with her uncle in his barge on Virginia Water, or visiting his menagerie at the Sandpit Gate. And for all his faults it was he who presided over the last great building programme at Windsor and he whose discriminating taste enhanced the royal collections with many fine works of art. He died in the early hours of June 26, 1830 at Windsor, unloved and unmourned by his people. Even before his body was in its grave Lady Conyngham had left the Castle, accompanied, so the gossips said, with wagon-loads of loot.

Prelude and Imperial Theme By contrast with his brother, William IV, who now became king, had enjoyed years of happy family life – with his mistress, the actress Mrs Jordan, and their numerous children. By the summer of 1831 Windsor was, in the words of one contemporary, 'quite full of *toute la bâtardise*'. Bluff, tactless and stupid, William prided himself on his connections with the Navy and relished his popular nickname of the Sailor King. He arrived at Windsor not only with his illegitimate children and their spouses but also with a wife, now Queen Adelaide, of 12 years standing. Many courtiers thought her even more awful than Lady Conyngham, but she was good-hearted enough, happy to do her knitting of an evening while her husband slept in his chair, waking only for dinner, when the band played.

'A weak, ignorant, commonplace sort of person' according to one of his obituaries, King Billy had no time for his brother's 'damned expensive taste' in 'knicknackery', and presented a collection of miscellaneous artistic treasures to the nation. He pulled down most of Royal Lodge and sent the menagerie to London Zoo.

William loved being king. He reopened the terraces and drives, and Windsor Home Park, to the public and even allowed public access to the royal apartments. Wrote one delighted visitor: 'Their majesties are accessible at all hours, the apartments are open to everybody: there is no seclusion, no mystery, nothing to conceal.' To celebrate his first birthday as king he threw a great party at Windsor; 100 guests sat down to dine in St George's Hall and 3,000 at trestle tables in the Long Walk. The king made a 'very good speech', a rare achievement for him, and the banquet seems to have been a considerable success. On another, and for those present highly embarrassing occasion, the king roundly insulted the Duchess of Kent, mother of the young Princess Victoria, claiming she was trying to keep her daughter from court.

In fact, according to court rumour, the duchess hoped that the king would die before her daughter came of age, allowing her to rule for a time as regent. The king disappointed her hopes by four weeks, dying barely a month after Victoria celebrated her 18th birthday at Windsor.

Home of Queen and Empress
Ironically, perhaps, it was Lord Conyngham, together with the Archbishop of Canterbury, who in June 1837 rode helter-skelter from Windsor to Kensington Palace to tell Victoria she was queen. After 40 years of rule by old men, England had a lively and pretty young woman as monarch. When at Windsor she loved to ride at full gallop in the Great Park after mornings devoted to state business and gossip with her beloved prime minister, Lord Melbourne. The middle-aged peer was undoubtedly dazzled by his young sovereign whom popular rumour dubbed 'Mrs Melbourne'. Victoria, who from the first had a strong sense of her own dignity, was incensed by the canard, and court protocol was more strict than it had been under her uncle. But she, like him, loved the job of monarch, and these were carefree happy times. On state occasions, the cares of business ended with glittering balls in the Red Drawing Room, the queen dancing until 3am surrounded by the stars and uniforms and pirouetting gowns of courtiers and visiting dignitaries.

It was at Windsor, in the year 1839, that she met the studious and handsome Prince Albert of Saxe-Coburg-Gotha. On the fourth day of his visit the queen had made up her mind. The following morning, certain, as she later confided to her aunt the Duchess of Gloucester, that he would 'never have presumed . . . to propose to the Queen of England', she summoned him to her little Blue Boudoir. Trembling, so she said, Victoria propositioned the Prince. Though reluctant to quit his happy little German princely court for the untidy turbulence of Europe's greatest royal family, Albert nobly accepted. With the stiffest of upper lips he reflected that 'with true resolution and zeal' he could not fail 'to continue noble, manly and princely in all things.' He was to need all his resolution in his future role.

From the first Victoria doted on her husband, but she refused him any more exalted title than 'Prince Consort' and for years denied him access to state papers. Their honeymoon at Windsor was virtually a public event, an inauspicious start to what was to become the model of royal family life. In fact, Albert soon came to love the Castle, finding in it the kind of scope for his young talents that a small German court would have offered. He began the business of cataloguing and ordering the superb collections of works of art and archives and set the farms running at a profit.

The locals objected to this injection of efficiency, just as the nation was always ready to resent any intervention by this German princeling in British affairs. In fact he was the most talented and conscientious royal to reside at Windsor since the days of Elizabeth I. When he died of typhoid in the Blue Room in 1861, even the British were beginning to recognize, grudgingly, his merits. It has been said that the Castle killed him; essential works on the drains had been left hanging for years, and the noxious air must have had an adverse effect on the constitution of the Prince, already weakened by the long hours of work he had devoted to his duties.

The Widow of Windsor The queen left Windsor for Osborne on the Isle of Wight rather than attend the funeral. When she returned she ordered that the prince's room be left untouched – for years, a manservant laid out a fresh suit in his dressing room and put a jug of warm water on the wash-stand. In fact, the queen's mourning lasted so long and took such extreme forms that public opinion became increasingly hostile.

The prince's body was first laid to rest in the annexe at the east end of St George's Chapel, begun by Henry VII. Victoria had the interior lined with marble and the building renamed as the Albert Memorial Chapel; meanwhile she ordered the building of a special mausoleum in Frogmore. Here the queen herself was to be buried at Albert's side. She was so obsessed by her dead husband that when their son, Edward Prince of Wales, was married to Princess Alexandra of Denmark in March 1863, she could not bring herself to participate in the service in St George's Chapel, watching instead from the oaken casement installed by Henry VIII on the north side of the altar for his Queen Catherine to watch the ceremonies of the Order of the Garter.

The gaiety of the young queen had long since been overlaid by her strict sense of propriety and the serious demeanour of her husband. The Court Circular recorded in tones of dull solemnity the queen's most trivial doings, even informing its readers when: 'Her Majesty was most graciously pleased during her stay at Windsor to enjoy most excellent health and

Henry VIII Gate

spirits'. Visitors to the Castle found it 'lacking that sociability which makes the agreeableness of an English country house.' Guests had no common drawing room where they could relax, being expected to remain in their own apartments – even the billiard room was so remote that it might as well have been in the town. Dinner time, the one occasion in the day when socializing was possible, was dominated by the 'sonorous tunes' of a military band.

There had of course always been entertainments and great occasions. In February 1853 a London company gave a performance of *Macbeth* in the Rubens Room; during the Ascot Races the royal party and guests enjoyed magnificent banquets off gold plate; when the French Emperor Napoleon III and his Empress Eugénie came to England in 1855, Windsor was the scene of a brilliant reception; and on less formal occasions there were parlour games and country dancing. At Christmas, the chandeliers in the queen's private sitting-room were taken down and Christmas trees aglow with candles hung in their place. As Albert observed with pleasure 'everything was German and *gemütlich*'. If the lake at Frogmore froze over in a hard winter the prince, a stylish skater, delighted to give his admiring family an exhibition. After his death happiness was banished from court and the queen became a recluse.

Affairs of State Public opinion grew restive, and for a time talk of republicanism became almost respectable. People grumbled that the queen was hardly earning her keep, while the familiarity with which she treated her Highland gillie, John Brown, gave rise to worse scandal. When the court was at Windsor his bedroom was only a few doors from hers; gossips found a new nickname for the Queen – 'Mrs Brown'. When told about this in later life Victoria remarked, smiling, 'I had no idea I was so notorious.' At times, the Queen's hermit-like existence seemed even to threaten Britain's relations with foreign powers – it was only with great reluctance that she agreed to a state visit from the Tsar of Russia. In the event, his reception at Windsor was a success while, despite initial apprehensions, the Queen positively enjoyed the visits of the Shah of Persia and the Sultan of Turkey, both installed at Windsor as Knights of the Garter. She was obviously delighted when the Shah told her he had ordered a translation into Persian of her *Journal of a Life in the Highlands*. She entertained him with bagpipes at lunch and took him on a personal tour of the Castle.

Court life could be arduous. Mealtime conversation was conducted in whispers; maids of honour might not entertain a man, even their brother, in their own rooms; young courtiers of either sex who had the audacity to get engaged were sure to incur the queen's displeasure. Smoking was permitted only in the remote billiard room; a German nobleman, rather than make the trek but desperate for a smoke, lay on

his back in his bedroom blowing the cigar smoke up the chimney. Courtiers, even ministers of state, smartly concealed themselves behind trees when they saw the queen's pony chair approaching them in the Park as Victoria, as she grew old, objected to being 'stared at'. But the old lady was kindly to those of her close family circle and the walls of her apartments were covered with pictures and photographs which followed her on her moves between Balmoral, Osborne and Windsor.

Victoria, the longest reigning monarch in the history of England, celebrated her Golden Jubilee in 1887, and her Diamond Jubilee a decade later. On the latter occasion the Queen Empress, known to her English subjects as the Widow of Windsor, received many of the

Max Beerbohm's cartoon of 'the rare, the rather awful visits of Albert Edward, Prince of Wales, to Windsor Castle'

royal guests come to do her homage at the Castle. Three years later she was serenaded by boys from Eton with patriotic songs in the upper quadrangle in celebration of the Relief of Mafeking in the Boer War. She continued to sign state papers to within ten days of her death at the Castle in January 1901, in the arms of her grandson, Wilhelm II, Kaiser of Germany.

Edwardian Windsor The Kaiser's affection for his grandmother was genuine; but a few days later, waiting for the beginning of the funeral cortege through the cobbled streets of Windsor, he shared in a little gesture of truly 'Edwardian' liberation with his fellow monarchs King Carlos of Portugal and Leopold King of the Belgians, all three puffing expansively at

The Royal Mausoleum, Frogmore, with the tomb of Queen Victoria and Prince Albert; from a painting by Brewer, 1869

their cigars 'by a fireplace in a corridor in Windsor Castle'.

King Edward's renowned bonhomie seems something of a miracle in view of his strict, often repressive upbringing and his mother's life-long suspicion and frequent hostility. Yet there had been happy days, following the Windsor buckhounds and shooting over the Castle coverts. Ironically, even here the earnest Prince Albert outshone him; Edward was never such a good shot as his father.

Within weeks of his mother's death, the 60-year-old monarch was making a grand sweep of pictures and treasured knick-knacks which had kept their hallowed places in the royal palaces for decades. At Windsor he cleared the mausoleum-like room of Prince Albert to dispel the brooding presence of his mother's extravagant mourning. To one observer of Edward's arrival at Windsor his court seemed a 'charming circle of cavaliers'. The quiet courts hummed to the motors of smart limousines, coach houses were converted into garages, new telephone lines were installed and the king, hatted, with stick in hand and dog on leash, marched through the rooms supervising a complete refit and redecoration. The hush of dinnertime was a thing of the past, and the old queen's household servants were given paid notice of six months. Guest-lists including artists and successful merchants would have shocked her, and in 1903 the Waterloo Chamber witnessed the first ball at Windsor in 50 years. King Edward made it his business to restore the 'sociability' of an agreeable English country house, but insisted on proper decorum being observed in protocol respecting himself and Queen Alexandra. At dinner ladies must wear their tiaras, gentlemen court dress and decorations. No lady could retire to bed before the queen, no gentleman before the king.

The House of Windsor Heir to the throne by the death of his elder brother in the 1890s, George V came to the throne on his father's death in 1910 a reluctant monarch. At first he preferred the homely atmosphere of Sandringham and Balmoral to the grandeur of Windsor. When he did move in, he ordered that the Blue Room should be left just as it had been in his father's time – familiarity made for comfort. Elsewhere in the Castle changes were made under the direction of his stately Queen Mary, who prided herself as something of a connoisseur. She catalogued the royal collections in her private notebooks and loved to conduct her visitors on tours of the Castle, of which she considered herself 'custodian for the nation'. Her most famous contribution to the treasures of Windsor is the splendid Queen Mary's Dolls' House.

A traditionalist in everything, but particularly in dress, King George could not abide the modern fashions, detesting everything from turn-ups on men's trousers to the rising hemline of women's frocks. When Edward, his eldest son, arrived at the breakfast table one morning wearing 'cuffs' to his trousers the king, who considered no gentleman turned up his trousers except perhaps to cross a puddle, roared at him: 'Is it raining in *here*?' The queen, proud of her shapely legs, had one of her ladies wear a short dress to test the king's reaction. The King disapproved, and Queen Mary continued to wear ankle-length frocks till her death. But she was always in secret sympathy with, and perhaps envious of, other women. One Easter Bank Holiday at Windsor she became exasperated with the king's contemptuous comments on the dresses of the holiday visitors on the terrace below their open window and ordered him 'peremptorily' to be silent. Court life reverted once more to the domestic dullness familiar in the days of Victoria. During the Great War, sensitive to the German ancestry of the royal house, the king's advisers recommended a change of the family name. After much debate 'Windsor', with its long royal associations, was chosen. On hearing the news the German Kaiser drily observed: 'I look forward to attending the next performance of *The Merry Wives of Saxe-Coburg-Gotha*'.

Bitterly angry at the wartime xenophobia that had forced this change on him, King George was equally warmed and surprised by the evident love he inspired in his subjects as his reign progressed. His death plunged the nation into mourning, which was eased only by the high hopes placed in the dashing and intelligent Prince of Wales, who now succeeded as Edward VIII.

Abdication and after The notorious events of Edward's tragic and short reign have passed into history. The new king's fond hope that his private life could remain private had no doubt been encouraged by the seclusion he had enjoyed in the home he had made for himself in Fort Belvedere, 'a castellated conglomeration' of a house some six miles from the Castle, dating from George IV's time. Here, as Prince of Wales, Edward had supervised a stylish modernization and spent happy hours, saw and billhook in hand, clearing the undergrowth in the grounds. Here too, he held his weekend parties when Mrs Simpson and her husband were frequent guests. The day after announcing his decision to abdicate he moved from Fort Belvedere to the Royal Lodge; and it was from here, on the evening of December 11th, 1936, that he was driven to the Castle, where from his old rooms in the Augusta Tower he made his abdication broadcast to the nation.

When King George VI succeeded his brother there were those who wondered whether the monarchy would long survive. That it has triumphantly done so is due in no small part to George himself and his beloved queen, now Queen Elizabeth the Queen Mother. More than anything, perhaps, it was their steadfast and cheerful courage during the World War soon to engulf Europe that endeared them and the institution they represented to their people. The king and queen spent most of their days working in Buckingham Palace or touring the war-torn streets of London and other cities, but Windsor was their base. The palace gave way to the fortress – flower-beds became vegetable gardens, in tune with the national 'Dig for Victory' campaign; ack-ack batteries were sited on the castle slopes; air-raid shelters were improvised in the grounds and dungeons; troops drilled for combat in the wards; slit trenches were dug in the Park. In these surroundings Princess Elizabeth and Princess Margaret lived much of their childhood at Royal Lodge. At Christmas they helped write and act the pantomimes given by them and the children of the household staff in the Waterloo Chamber. In the last year of the war King George reluctantly yielded to the pleas of his elder daughter and the future queen was enrolled as Second Lieutenant Elizabeth Windsor in the Auxiliary Transport Service.

Two years before this, in 1943, a dashing young naval officer, Philip Mountbatten, had made his first appearance among the family and guests at Windsor. In 1947 Elizabeth and Philip were married, to the plaudits of a jubilant nation; in February 1960 the queen declared in Council that her descendants could bear the family name Mountbatten-Windsor.

The family aspect of life at Windsor was continued by Queen Elizabeth II when she came to the throne in 1952. Yet her work on state business is as carefully planned there as at her other residences. The red boxes of state papers are brought to her each day and dealt with systematically and thoroughly. The high ceremonials of the Order of the Garter are maintained with due pomp and ceremony and the great walls and splendid apartments of the ancient fortress-palace seem today as enduring a symbol of the British monarchy as they have ever been.

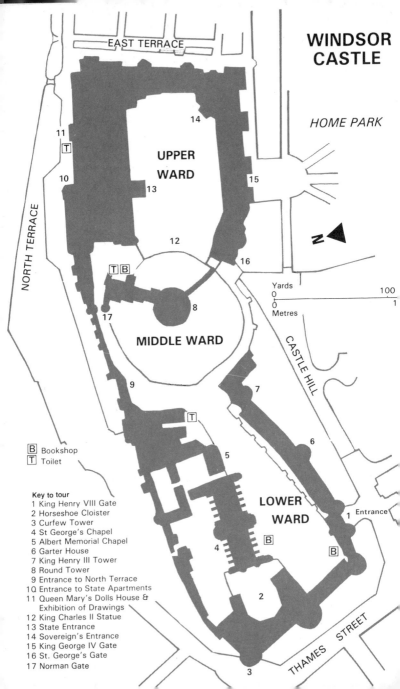

WINDSOR CASTLE

EAST TERRACE

HOME PARK

UPPER WARD

NORTH TERRACE

MIDDLE WARD

Yards
0   100
0   1
Metres

N

CASTLE HILL

LOWER WARD

Entrance

B Bookshop
T Toilet

Key to tour
1 King Henry VIII Gate
2 Horseshoe Cloister
3 Curfew Tower
4 St George's Chapel
5 Albert Memorial Chapel
6 Garter House
7 King Henry III Tower
8 Round Tower
9 Entrance to North Terrace
10 Entrance to State Apartments
11 Queen Mary's Dolls House &
   Exhibition of Drawings
12 King Charles II Statue
13 State Entrance
14 Sovereign's Entrance
15 King George IV Gate
16 St. George's Gate
17 Norman Gate

THAMES STREET

OPENING TIMES

Castle precincts open:
Daily, Jan-Mar & Nov-Dec 10-4.15;
Apr & Sep-Oct 10-5.15; May-Aug
10-7.15

Also open to the public

State Apartments
Jan-Mar & Nov-Dec, Mon-Sat 10.30-
3.15; Apr-Oct, Mon-Sat 10.30-3.15;
May-mid Oct also Sun 1.30-4.45. Last
admission ¼hr before closing. State
Apartments closed when HM The
Queen in residence. Entrance fee

Exhibition of Drawings
Times as for State Apartments.
Entrance fee

Queen Mary's Dolls' House
Times as for State Apartments.
Entrance fee

Curfew Tower
Tue-Sat 11-1 & 2-4 (last admission
¼hr before closing). Entrance fee

St George's Chapel
Apr-Oct, Mon-Sat 10.45-4, Sun 2-4;
Nov-Mar, Mon-Sat 10.45-3.45, Sun 2-
3.45. Entrance fee

Albert Memorial Chapel
Mon-Sat 10-1 & 2-3.45

Frogmore Gardens
Gardens and Mausoleum
Limited opening in early May (2 days,
11-7) in aid of National Gardens
Scheme (details from Tourist
Information Office). Also (Mausoleum
only) Wed nearest Queen Victoria's
birthday (May 26) 11-4

The Savill Gardens
Woodland and herbaceous gardens
Mon-Fri 10-6, Sat & Sun 10-7, or
dusk. Entrance fee

Valley Gardens
Woodland and heather gardens
Daily, 8-8 (or dusk)

Virginia Water
Lakeside woodlands and gardens

Events Changing of the Guard,
Windsor Castle (Mon-Sat am); Garter
Ceremony, St George's Chapel (Jun);
Royal Windsor Rose and Horticultural
Show, Windsor Castle grounds (Jul)

Tour of the Castle From Castle Hill in
Windsor town the Castle is entered by
the *King Henry VIII Gateway*, with the
arms of the monarch over the entrance
arch. The **Lower Ward** permits a view
of most of the Castle's important buildings. Ahead are the buttresses and
pinnacles of St George's Chapel, with
statues in their niches and the heraldic
Royal Beasts rearing to the sky. To the
W (left) of the Chapel lies the brick and
timber frame outer wall of the
Horseshoe Cloister, with the gable and
clock of the Curfew Tower rising behind it. E (right) of the Chapel can just
be seen the buttresses of the Albert
Memorial Chapel. Further up the hill
are the two towers of the Norman
Gateway and to the right of them the
great Round Tower rises above its
mound – if the Royal Standard is
flying, the Queen is in residence.

Now head across the Parade Ground
for the archway entrance to the
Horseshoe Cloister. Built in the 1480s,
though much restored in the late 19th
c., it houses the comfortable apartments for the men (lay clerks) of St
George's Chapel. Opposite is the
Chapel's grand *W front*, its magnificent window flanked by corner turrets
and the ogee roofs of the Beaufort and
Urswick chantry chapels. The W door,
open on ceremonial occasions, is approached by a wide staircase built in the
1870s.

Behind the cloister (W corner) is the
Curfew Tower, originally 13th-c.,
which has a medieval dungeon and
secret underground exit in the basement. The gabled top storey contains
the eight bells of St George's Chapel,
chimed every three hours. The tour is
continued through a second archway
up the steps to the area known as
Denton Commons. On your left is the
15th-c. *Chapter Library*, to the right
buildings housing members of the
Chapel establishment. From the terrace overlooking the outer wall of the
Castle there is a lovely view of Eton
College Chapel beyond the Thames.
Now return to the Parade Ground and
turn left up the path in the Lower

The Choir, St George's Chapel

Ward for the entrance to the Chapel in the porch built into the angle between the nave and the S transept.

A fee is charged for entry to **St George's Chapel**, but do not miss this marvellous building. Architecturally it is unusual in that the transepts are central, but once you are inside this magical interior such technical considerations are secondary. The lofty arcades are finely moulded, above them blank panelling and a carved frieze of angels support the windows of the clerestory. Over all soars the lovely and intricate vault, in which ribs splay fanwise to a coved ceiling of complex short ribs and heraldic bosses, many bearing the badge of Sir Reginald Bray (d. 1503) whose legacies financed the completion of the nave. Turn left up the *S aisle* to the *Beaufort Chantry* chapel. Behind the bronze screen can be seen the large marble *Tomb of Charles Somerset* (d. 1526), ancestor of the Dukes of Beaufort; a remarkable Jacobean *font* of wood, in the form of a covered drinking cup in blue and red and gilding; and, in a niche to the left, a mid-13th-c. Spanish *statue* of the Virgin and Child.

Cross the W end, pausing to admire the vista of the nave, broken halfway by a stone screen and divided organ case (1790s) over which the roof continues its majestic course. Now to the *Urswick Chantry* chapel, at the foot of the N aisle. On the pillar to its left is an intriguing bronze *plate* commemorating the death in 1879 of Prince Alamaya, son of Emperor Theodore of Ethiopia. The 18-year-old Prince was staying at Windsor as a guest of Queen Victoria when he died. Above the plate is the Lion of Ethiopia, below the George and Dragon badge of the Order of the Garter. A silver label was rivetted across the plate to record the visit of another member of the Abyssinian royal house to Windsor in the 1920s.

The chantry itself was built for a courtier of Henry VII, but today is dominated by the soaring marble *Monument to Princess Charlotte*, beloved only child of King George IV, who died in childbirth in 1824. Flanked by mourning women and angels, the body of the Princess lies on a slab, the fingers of one hand visible beneath the shroud which drapes her. Above, her transfigured body flanked by angels (the left-hand one bearing the still-born baby) rises heavenwards.

In the next bay between N aisle and nave stands the *Tomb of King George V and Queen Mary*. Continuing along the aisle, the N transept is reached: this is the *Rutland Chantry* chapel. It is reserved for prayer and closed to the visitor, but through the stone screen (*c.* 1500) can be seen the superb alabaster

Monument to Lord Roos (d. 1513) and his wife. In the late Middle Ages English alabaster work had a European reputation and this monument, an interesting blend of medieval conventions and early Renaissance forms, is one of the finest examples. Niches round the tomb chest, beneath the recumbent figures, house mourning knights and ladies, and angels bearing heraldic shields. Next comes the little *Memorial Chapel and Tomb of King George VI* (d. 1952).

Three bays along the *N chancel aisle*, on the right, is the *Hastings Chantry* chapel to Lord Hastings (d. 1483) with early 16th-c. wall paintings of the Martyrdom of St Stephen. Ahead, the roof of the aisle drops to accommodate the stone wall and oriel window of the chantry chapel built for Edward IV. Below is the late 18th-c. Gothick wall monument to the king.

On your left, as you enter the **choir**, is the exquisite *wrought-iron grille* made in the 1480s by the master smith John Tresilian for the tomb of King Edward IV. It is a fine and delicate filigree, topped by elegant turreted pinnacles. On the opposite side of the choir is the white marble *Tomb of King Edward VII* (d. 1910) and *Queen `Alexandra*. The gilded alabaster *reredos* was erected in the 1860s as a memorial to Prince Albert, and the *E window* above it rebuilt at the same time. In the N chancel wall to your left are two *oriels*. The stone one over the arch was built for the Edward IV Chantry chapel in the 1480s (the chantry was transformed into a royal pew in the 18th c., reserved for the queen and the ladies of court). The wooden oriel to the right was added by Henry VIII so, it is said, that Queen Catherine could watch the ceremonies of the Order of the Garter. (From here, still in mourning for Albert, Queen Victoria watched the wedding of her son, later Edward VII). Topped by a profusion of gilded and painted badges and heraldic animals, the arches, panelling and balusters of the window combine Gothic and Renaissance elements.

The *chancel stalls* are one of the glories of medieval wood carving. Above them hang the resplendent heraldic banners of the present members of the Order of the Garter, for whose predecessors this magnificent choir was built. Created between 1478 and 1485 under the direction of master carver William Berkeley, the stalls are ranged on either side of the chancel in three tiers; at the back are those of the Knights of the Garter, the dean and canons; below them come the Military Knights and the choirmen; and below them the choir boys. The Garter Knight stalls are surmounted by elaborate canopies topped by strange little manikin heads designed to carry the knights' helms and heraldic accoutrements. The seats of the stalls are carved on their underside with misericords but, apart from the two on either side of the centre of the chancel, these cannot be seen as the stalls are roped off. The back of each stall is adorned with the heraldic brasses of the members of the Order who have occupied it. The oldest of these stall plates is that of *Lord Basset* (*c.* 1390) in the eighth stall from the W end and on the S side. The large brass *lectern* is early 16th-c. Continental work and the two *slabs* let into the floor of the chancel mark the burials of Kings George III and IV and William IV, in the royal vault below, and of Henry VIII and Charles I.

The Royal stalls are at the W end of the choir, those of the Queen and Prince Philip on the left, the Prince of Wales and Queen Elizabeth The Queen Mother on the right. The Queen's stall, being that of the Sovereign of the Order, is distinguished with a large canopy and by the fact that it has no stall plates. The *misericord* of the Queen's stall depicts the signing of the Treaty of Picquigny between King Edward V and Louis XI of 1475, in which Louis bought off a massive and well-equipped invasion force taken over to France by Edward with the guarantee of a large annual pension which was paid until Edward's death. A replica of this unique carving is outside the choir.

Leaving the choir between the royal stalls, pause to admire the *W window*, done in the early 16th c. and depicting kings and church figures. To the left, in the polygonal S transept, is the *Bray Chantry* chapel. Dedicated to Sir Reginald Bray (d. 1503), St George's Chapel's great benefactor, it contains many interesting monuments, including one to the son of Emperor Napoleon III of France. Leaving the Bray Chantry and entering the *S chancel aisle* you pass, on the right, the little *Chapel of Bishop Oliver King* (d. 1503), Royal Secretary in four reigns. Diagonally across the S aisle hangs the great two-handed *sword of King Edward III*. Next to this is the *Oxenbridge Chantry* with its early 16th-c. panel painting of the death of St John the Baptist.

On the last bay of the choir wall notice the Garter *stall plate* of Thomas Howard, 4th Duke of Norfolk. In 1572 he was executed for treasonable plotting with Mary, Queen of Scots, stripped of his honours and his Garter plate removed from the Chapel; it was recovered in the 1950s and placed here in the precincts, as it were, of the Order of which he was once a member. Next to it stands a fascinating iron 15th-c. *alms box* with four locks in the lid and 20 coin slots in castle-like turrets, lid and centrepiece. The letters H on it no doubt stand for Henry VI, whose body was transferred from Chertsey Abbey in 1484 on orders of Richard III to the place now marked by a black slab, once the site of a pilgrim shrine to the saintly king.

Passing the *Tomb of Edward VII and Queen Alexandra* notice the king's favourite dog, Caesar, at his feet. Diagonally across the aisle is the *Lincoln Chantry* chapel with its 15th-c. iron grille and alabaster monument to Edward, Earl of Lincoln (d. 1585). The chantry was built by Edward IV to house the relics of John Schorne, a Buckingham priest (d. 1314) renowned as a healer whose presence, the king hoped, would bring pilgrims to his new foundation. In the ambulatory which leads across the E end of the Chapel

W front, St George's Chapel

grille ornamented in *art nouveau* style. The *Tomb of Leopold, Duke of Albany* (d. 1884) Queen Victoria's youngest son, is at the W end, the marble *Cenotaph to Prince Albert* at the E end. The Consort's body lies in the mausoleum at Frogmore.

Leaving the Albert Memorial Chapel, you find the great **Round Tower** looming ahead. Despite its name, it is not a perfect circle. The lower storeys date from *c* 1180, the large Gothic-style windows and the storeys above them and the machicolation were added by Wyatville. Almost opposite the Chapel across the Lower Ward is the 13th-c. **Henry III Tower**; the range of buildings between this and the Henry VIII Gateway house the quarters of the Garter Military Knights. The path skirting the Castle mound to the right leads to *St George's Gate* and beside it the entrance to the *Moat Path*, which when open offers full view of the Quadrangle in the Upper Ward. The path is not always open. Head towards the *Norman Gate* (the right tower *c.* 1350, the left, Wyatville) but take the gate in the wall for the *North Terrace*. Here, there are splendid panoramic views across the Thames to Eton College Chapel beyond. The precipitous drop from below the Terrace wall is a reminder of Windsor's strategic strength. A door from the Terrace gives access to: the **Royal Collection of Drawings**, one of the world's finest with work by most of the great masters of western art from the Renaissance; and to **Queen Mary's Dolls' House**, with its beautiful miniature fittings and period furniture.

The Terrace continues beyond the E front of the Castle to overlook the *Sunken Garden* by Wyatville. When the Royal Family is not in residence this may be open to the public; beneath the terrace from which you view the garden, the former *Orangery* is now a gymnasium. Now return to the North Terrace entrance for the visit to the State Apartments. Guided tours of the apartments are not permitted, and visitors must follow the fixed itinerary.

notice the 19th-c. spiral staircase and next to it the beautiful 13th-c. *door* (the original W door to King Henry III's Chapel) with its exquisite contemporary iron-work signed *Gilebertus*.

Leaving St George's Chapel by the end of the N aisle you come to the 14th-c. *Dean's Cloister*; down the passage from the SW corner (left), is the magnificent 14th-c. *porch of honour*, one of the most important architectural features of the Chapel.

Retrace your steps through the cloisters to the passage opposite for the **Albert Memorial Chapel** (closed 1-2). There is a fine 13th-c. painted *portrait head* to the right of the door showing that this wall existed at the time of Henry III who built the first chapel on this site. However, Henry's chapel was almost entirely rebuilt in reconstructions under Edward III, Henry VIII and Cardinal Wolsey (the vault) and then transformed in appearance by renovations ordered by Queen Victoria. The interior space is now dominated by a massive bronze and marble *Monument to the Duke of Clarence* (d. 1892), son and heir of Edward Prince of Wales. An angel holds a crown above the head of the recumbent prince, and the whole monument is surrounded by an iron

The Grand Staircase

State Apartments Entering from the terrace you ascend to a hall lined with a display of the *Royal Porcelain*. From here the Gothic **Grand Staircase** (Anthony Salvin, 1866) illuminated by its lantern windows, provides a dramatic entrance. The staircase is dominated by a marble *statue of King George IV* (by Sir Francis Chantrey) beneath which stands a huge *suit of armour* made for Henry VIII at the Royal Armouries in Greenwich in 1540. Either side of the staircase two other suits of armour are displayed on life-size model horses, and the walls of the staircase, like those of the vestibule it leads to, are lined or hung with armour, swords and weapons of every kind. (The temporary footbridge crossing the staircase is dismantled when the Queen is in residence). The **Grand Vestibule**, vaulted by James Wyatt in the 1790s, was the staircase hall at that time. At one end is a seated *statue of Queen Victoria* (1871) under a Gothic canopy. The display cabinets contain swords and firearms and trophies; in the side window of the one by the fireplace on the right you can see the sniper's bullet 'by which Nelson was killed', mounted in a little silver case, inside the lid of which can be seen the original identification paper tag with its faded inscription. To the right of the Grand Vestibule is the Queen's Guard Room, which you come to later in the itinerary.

Ahead is the **Waterloo Chamber**, built in the 1820s on the orders of George IV to house portraits of leaders of the victorious allies against Napoleon. Most of the paintings are by Sir Thomas Lawrence. The great room fills one of the former courtyards of the palace, and is lit by ranges of windows down either side of the lofty timber roof. Opposite the entrance from the Grand Vestibule, Lawrence's great portrait of the Duke of Wellington holding the Sword of State dominates the room, with, on his left, his ally the Prussian Field Marshal Blücher. Over the fireplace can be seen George III, flanked on his left by George IV and on his right by William IV. Above the panelling the wall is filled by astonishing Victorian fretwork; a strange contrast to the exquisite wood carving in the panels which was salvaged from the work done by Grinling Gibbons for a chapel demolished in Wyatville's reconstructions.

Next on the itinerary comes the **Garter Throne Room**; this too has Grinling Gibbons carvings from the vanished chapel. Part of Wyatville's restorations, the room occupies one of the oldest parts of the Castle. At the far end is the sovereign's throne, and over the fireplace James Gunn's portrait of Queen Elizabeth II as sovereign of the order. To her left are Prince Albert and Queen Victoria in their garter robes (by Winterhalter), and the portraits of England's monarchs from George I to William IV occupy the other panels. Continue into the **Grand Reception Room**, with gilded decor by Wyatville

in rococo mood. The 18th-c. Gobelins tapestries are on the theme of Jason and the Golden Fleece; the room is lit by elaborate chandeliers and lined with gilt chairs upholstered in 18th-c. French tapestry; in the window is a huge green malachite vase presented to Queen Victoria by Tsar Nicholas I of Russia; the chinoiserie clock and barometer above the fireplaces came from the Brighton Pavilion.

You now come to the **St George's Hall**. 185ft long, it is almost twice the length it was in King Charles II's time. The W half (to your left) was occupied by a superb baroque chapel by Hugh May, from which little but the Grinling Gibbons carvings was salvaged. May's dramatic scheme of decoration for the hall itself, which dates back to the reign of Edward III, was also done away with in Wyatville's restored Gothic scheme. The walls are lined with portraits and stands of armour, below which a stone frieze carries shields bearing the coats of arms of members of the Order of the Garter. Similar shields line the timber roof, so that all the members of the Order since its foundation in the 1340s are represented. The great hall is still in regular use for state banquets.

Next comes the **Queen's Guard Chamber**, lit by three windows in the area above the porte cochère of the Quadrangle. In the centre stands a mounted and armoured figure representing the King's Champion, an honour long held by members of the Dimmock family, who rode fully armed into the coronation banquet of each new sovereign to challenge any present who might deny the sovereign's title. On either side are busts of Marlborough (left) and Wellington (right) above which hang the old royal standard of France and the French tricolour, still rendered annually as token rent for their estates by the dukes' descendants.

You now enter the *Apartments* created by Hugh May for Charles II and his queen, Catharine of Braganza. Visitors to Queen Catharine, passing through the Queen's Guard Chamber, were admitted to the first room, the **Queen's Presence Chamber**. Notice the superb carving by Gibbons and his assistants, notably Henry Phillips, and the painted ceiling by the Italian Antonio Verrio, depicting the Queen surrounded by the Virtues and the figure of Time. The tapestries are 18th-c. Gobelins work; the marble fireplace, designed by Robert Adam, was originally in Buckingham Palace.

From the Presence Chamber visitors were admitted to the **Queen's Audience Chamber**, where Queen Catharine received them. Here Verrio's painted ceiling depicts her seated in a chariot drawn by swans towards the Temple of Virtue. Once again there is a handsome 18th-c. fireplace and superb carvings by Gibbons; also notice the Japanese lacquer cabinets on early 18th-c. English gilt wood stands. The **Queen's Ball Room**, which comes next, was remodelled in the early 1800s, the ceiling by Wyatville. The paintings include Van Dyck's famous portrait of Charles I's children and portraits by the American artists Benjamin West and John Singleton Copley for George III. The **Queen's Drawing Room** (another Wyatville interior) has many paintings by Van Dyck, and some outstanding 17th-c. chairs. The **King's Closet** (named for Charles II) has a magnificent silver table and mirror set presented to William III and three paintings by Hans Holbein the Younger, notably that of Sir Henry Guildford close to the exit. Next is the **King's Dressing Room**, another interior designed by Hugh May and remodelled by Wyatville. The room has another silver mirror and table, this one presented to Charles II, and a stunning wealth of paintings; the most famous, no doubt, the triple head of King Charles I by Van Dyck. There are also portraits by Holbein, Dürer, Rembrandt, Rubens and, in the centre of the long wall, *The Music Lesson* by Jan Vermeer.

The **King's State Bedchamber**, so called since the days of Charles II,

The King's Drawing Room

though he actually slept elsewhere, is lined with paintings by Canaletto. The bed was installed here in 1855 for the state visit of the French Emperor Napoleon III and his Empress Eugenie. There are many fine paintings by Rubens in the **King's Drawing Room**, and the itinerary ends with the **King's Dining Room**, one of the most marvellous in the whole suite. Once again the carving is by Gibbons and Phillips: the ceiling, which depicts a Banquet of the Gods, if a little lugubrious, is a colourful piece of decor and the marble fireplace with its classical columns is late 18th-c. This is the last of the three Hugh May interiors to survive at Windsor, but it is now somewhat dark because the windows had to be blocked off when Salvin built his staircase.

Leaving the State Apartments across the staircase via the footbridge, pause for a moment to enjoy the great stairwell and, especially perhaps, the Henry VIII armour below George IV's statue. You emerge from the Castle on the State Apartment itinerary through the *King John Tower* into a small courtyard. On the left are railings from which the *Quadrangle* of the **Upper Ward** may be viewed. A 1670s *equestrian statue* of Charles II, with reliefs by Grinling Gibbons around its base, surveys the scene. To your left is the grand porte cochère entrance to the State Apartments, diagonally opposite the *Sovereign's Entrance* to the private royal apartments. Now return to the **Middle Ward** of the Castle through the *Norman Gateway*, noting the door to the Governor's Apartments on your left before you leave, and the exciting skyline of the royal beasts of St George's Chapel down the hill.

Windsor Great Park
See map, p.91

Access to the Long Walk (pedestrians) from George IV Gate or Park Street. Access by car on A332 (parking on W side). Other car parks: Savill Gardens, Valley Gardens and S side of Park.

Leaving Windsor by the A332 for Ascot, you come to the first public entrance to Windsor Great Park, some 5000 acres of woodland, farmland and grassy glades among the grees. Although only a short distance from the town it offers beautiful, secluded walks and picnic areas. The remains of the great royal forest, once reserved for the monarch's hunting, the park is now almost wholly open to the public. A favourite place of pilgrimage is the *Copper Horse* which stands on Snow Hill, for it was here in July 1977 that Queen Elizabeth II lit the great bonfire, the first in a chain of beacons that spread throughout Great Britain to celebrate the Silver Jubilee of her reign. The Copper Horse, an equestrian statue of King George III in Roman toga, was erected in 1831. In July 1981 it was the scene of another bonfire to mark the wedding of Prince Charles to Lady Diana Spencer. The site has magnificent views over the Great Park and the *Long Walk*, the 3m avenue which leads from it to the King George IV Gateway of Windsor Castle. On the E edge of the Great Park lie the Savill Gardens, and to the SE Virginia Water and the Valley Gardens.

The Savill Gardens

E side of Windsor Great Park. Access from Wick Lane (S of Old Windsor) or Wick Road (off A30). Car park

Laid out between 1932 and 1949 by Sir Eric Savill, Deputy Ranger of Windsor Great Park, the gardens cover 35 acres of woodland and valley glades. Beds of daffodils and lilies are the main feature of the spring; as the year advances ornamental trees and shrubs of all varieties come into their own, the rhododendrons, camellias, magnolias and hydrangeas being especially noteworthy. The summer garden of roses, and the herbaceous borders which flourish in the moist woodland conditions, are

The Long Walk, Windsor Castle

laid out more formally. There are also alpines and a dry garden. There is a restaurant (open Mar-Oct), and a well-stocked plant shop. The entrance is well signposted from Ascot, Egham, Windsor and Old Windsor. Dogs are not allowed, and visitors are requested not to picnic in the Gardens.

Valley Gardens and Virginia Water

S side of Windsor Great Park. Access from Savill Garden, or from Wick Road (or A30). Car park

Covering some 400 acres on the N banks of Virginia Water lake, the development of the site as a garden began in 1949. Scrub and undergrowth were cleared but many of the beech, oaks, sweet chestnuts and other trees survive to make this one of the world's most beautiful woodland gardens. Acres of meadow are bright with daffodils in the spring, while adjacent to the main garden is a heather garden of some 10 acres, and a large area devoted to dwarf and slow-growing conifers. The main Gardens are rich in flowering trees and shrubs in almost unequalled profusion and diversity. To the S lies *Virginia Water*, a lake some 120 acres in extent, laid out and excavated in the mid-18th c. and later adorned with the *Ruins*, fragments of the ancient Roman city of Leptis Magna in Libya.

Home Park

To the N, E and S of Windsor Castle, N of Windsor Great Park

Near the N end of the Long Walk is Frogmore, the creation of George III's queen, Charlotte, who acquired the property in the 1790s and made it into a royal retreat. *Frogmore House* is a re-building by Wyatt of the original house: empty since the last war, it is not open to the public. *Frogmore Gardens*, however, can be visited on two days in early May. Also open at this time, and on the Wednesday nearest to Queen Victoria's birthday (May 26) is the *Royal Mausoleum*, final resting place of Queen Victoria and Prince Albert. (The Mausoleum is also the burial place of the Duke of Windsor, formerly Edward VIII). Another interesting feature at Frogmore is the *Prince Consort's Home Farm*, where Albert built a model dairy.

Gazetteer

EC: Early Closing MD: Market Day
Populations over 10,000 shown
Map references after place names
refer to map inside back cover.
Information centres listed offer a
tourist accommodation booking service

This includes information
on the location, history and
main features of the places
of interest in the region.
Visiting hours for all places
open to the public are shown
in 'The Best of the Region'.
Asterisks indicate references
to other Gazeteer entries.
(NT) indicates ownership
by the National Trust.

Interior, Milton's Cottage

Amersham   D1
Bucks. Pop 17,254. 14m N of Windsor (A355/
A413/A404/A416). EC Thur

The glories of Amersham are the High
Street, one of the prettiest in southern
England, and the monument to Henry
Curwen in St Mary's Church. Surrounded by woods along the little River
Misbourne, the place grew as a market
and a centre for woodworking. During
the 17th c. Amersham was something
of a focus of religious dissent, and the
Martyrs' Memorial in the fields behind
Station Road commemorates the persec-
utions they suffered. *Bury Farm* at the
foot of Gore Hill was the home of Guil-
ielma Springett who married William
Penn, founder of Pennsylvania.

Approaching   from   Beaconsfield
(A355) or Chalfont St Giles (A413) you
will find parking E of the church and
the delightful *Memorial Gardens* with
flowerbeds, lawns and cross focussed
on fountain and pond. The large **St
Mary's Church** with its W tower
embellished by stair turret and spirelet
is basically 13th- and 15th-c. work,
much restored in the 1890s and the
20th c. It has been refloored throughout in polished composite stone tiles,
the statues gilded and repainted and
the interior cleaned and spruced up
like an elegant museum. In the 16th c.
the Scottish reformer John Knox
preached here.

The church has a vaulted porch, and
fantastically carved heads in the roof
corbels. In the N aisle four medieval
brasses have been tidily laid out on the
new flooring; they include those to
Henry Brudenell and his wife (*c.* 1430).
There are some fine wall monuments,
most notably the *Curwen memorial* on
the N wall of the chancel. Of creamy
grey-white alabaster, sparingly but
beautifully embellished with gilding on
the hair of the figures and other details,
it commemorates young Henry Curwen (d. 1636) 'onely sonne of Sir Patri-
cius Curwen of Workington in the
County of Cumberland, Baronet and
the Lady Isabella his wife.' The epi-
taph tells a story of grief mingled with
dynastic tragedy, both characteristic of

its age and deeply moving. It continues: 'Descended from the noble family of the Gospatricks Earls of Northumberland and of his house the 23rd in lineal descent since the Conquest, he was sent hither to be instructed in learning under the tuition of Charles Croke D.D. and Rector of this church, wherein having proceeded to the love and admiration of all who knew him at 14 years of age he deceased, leaving his absent parents full of sorrow whose love doth thus express itself in the sad memory of him, whereto they have dedicated this monument.' Above stands the near life-size figure of Learning flanked by mourning allegorical figures and on either side of the pediment the figures of Grammar and Arithmetic.

From the churchyard you can see the lantern of the old **Market Hall** (1628). The building is raised on arches above an open ground storey and the old double lock-up. *The Crown Hotel*, much restored, contains 16th-c. wall paintings and a fire-damaged royal coat-of-arms of the period with lion and dragon supporters; it may commemorate a visit of Queen Elizabeth I to *Shardeloes*, a 16th-c. mansion ¾m W of the town.

Continue up **High Street**, which despite the heavy traffic has a pervading air of gentle calm, flanked by its modest mellow red-brick cottages and houses. Up from the *Market Hall* on the left stands the half-timbered range of the 15th-16th-c. *King's Arms*; further up on the other side the low gables of *The Elephant and Castle* and *Severn House*, its columned doorway framed in a neat arch of yew hedge. Towards the end of the street notice the charming 17th-c. brick *Almshouses* ranged round a court, the buildings terminating in blind classical arches. Mill Lane, on the right, leads down to the river, which once drove the mill and now skirts the cricket ground. Little plank 'bridges' link this with the back garden gates, among them that of *The Eagle Inn*, an ideal place for a pint if your visit coincides with a cricket match.

Ascot C3
Berks. Village on A329/A330/A332 7m S of Windsor. Event: Royal Ascot Week (3rd week in Jun). EC Wed

Racing was inaugurated here in 1711 by Queen Anne in preference to Datchet Mead, where Charles II had 'appointed horse races to be run.' After her death interest in the meeting lapsed. It was revived by the Duke of Cumberland, and by the end of the 18th c. royalty were frequent visitors. The Ascot Royal Cup was first presented in 1807 and Royal Ascot, held in the third week of June, has long been one of the great events in the British social calendar. The races are regularly graced by the presence of Her Majesty The Queen and other members of the Royal Family, who ride down the course in open landaus. Admission to the royal enclosure is by ticket, and for most of those present the activities on the race course are a secondary diversion to the important business of fashion and extravagant picnic hamper lunches. It is said, by those who care about such matters, that even the Royal Enclosure has lost its exclusive social cachet and is now about as eleagant and poised as a 'Mardi Gras'. The *Queen Elizabeth II Grandstand* and *Tattersalls Enclosure*, where the on-course bookies have their pitch, were built in 1961-4.

Basildon Park see *Goring & Streatley*

Beaconsfield C1
Bucks. Pop 11,700. 9m N of Windsor (M40/A40/ A355/B474). EC Wed, Sat

New Beaconsfield, ½m N of the main road, is the main centre of population, but the old village, focussed on the church at the crossroads, is a beautiful and opulent place, full of red brick with some comfortable and picturesque hostelries, good restaurants and numerous antique shops. It has many literary associations. Edmund Waller the poet built *Hall Barn*, still a private residence off Windsor End in 1660. In the late 18th c. Edmund Burke lived at a house since destroyed, where Sheridan, Garrick and Johnson were among

Boulter's Lock, Maidenhead

Great Hall, Dorney Court. Opposite: Burnham Beeches

his guests. Early in the 1800s William Hickey, the diarist, lived and wrote his boisterous memoirs at *Little Hall Barn* (also Windsor End). It was at *Overroads* in Grove Road, New Beaconsfield, that G.K. Chesterton lived for some 25 years up to 1935 and wrote the 'Father Brown' stories.

The roads which converge on the church are the four ancient 'Ends' of Beaconsfield. The A40 is London End as it runs E, Wycombe End as it runs W; northwards, Aylesbury End leads to New Beaconsfield and southwards Windsor End to the M4 motorway. The flint and Bath stone **Church of St Mary and All Saints** (mainly 19th-c.) contains a floor tablet to Edmund Burke (d. 1797), who is buried here, and the churchyard an obelisk monument to Edmund Waller (d. 1687). From the churchyard you can see the E-shaped *Old Rectory*, begun about 1500, and opposite the church lies the splendid range of *The Saracen's Head*, with its bars and grill rooms behind an impressive half-timbered facade.

In New Beaconsfield is the impressive **Bekonscot Model Village**, complete with its hand-carved population.

Bisham B2
Berks. Village off A404, 4½m NW of Maidenhead

Lying in a classic English rural setting between the Thames and rising wooded slopes, the delightful village is noted for the 16th-c. *Mansion* built by Sir Philip Hoby on the site of Bisham Abbey (founded and dissolved by Henry VIII) and for the treasure of monuments in the **Church of All Saints**. The tower proclaims the Norman origins of the building; the rest of the structure is heavily restored except for the 16th-c. *Hoby Chapel*. Of the four family tombs, that to Margaret Hoby (d. 1605) widow of Sir Edward Hoby, is the most remarkable. An obelisk surmounted by a heart is surrounded by four swans, an heraldic badge of the Carey family from which the lady came. The half brothers Sir Philip (d. 1558) and Sir Thomas Hoby (d. 1566) lie side by side in their alabaster

armour. Sir Thomas's widow, Elizabeth Hoby (d. 1609), later Lady Russell, is magnificently commemorated with her children behind her, kneeling beneath a canopy and wearing her coronet.

Boulter's Lock see *Maidenhead*

Bradenham (NT) C1
Bucks. Village off A4010, 5m NW of High Wycombe

The village was acquired by the National Trust in the 1950s. The gate piers of the large, dark red-brick 1670s *Manor House* overlook the green. From the 1820s to the 1840s it was the home of Isaac d'Israeli, whose son, Benjamin Disraeli (later prime minister) immortalized it as Hurstley in his novel *Endymion*. The flint and stone **St Botolph's Church**, heavily restored in the 1860s by G.E. Street, has a Norman S doorway, a 15th-c. tower and some interesting enamelled glass in the E window of the chapel. The huge wall monument, with its columns and pediment, life-size figures and cherubs, is to Charles West (d. 1684). Beech woods rise above the village.

Bray C2
Berks. Village on B3028, on S outskirts of Maidenhead

The parish, it is said, of the Vicar of Bray in the well-known song. Dating from the 18th c., the verses recount the parson's determination to remain vicar of Bray, by trimming to the changing religious views between the reigns of Charles II and George I. However, the original for the story may have been Simon Aleyn, the incumbent from the early 1540s to the 1580s. As vicar of Bray during the reigns of Henry VIII, Edward VI, Mary I and Elizabeth I (a period when the shifts of religious orthodoxies were far more fundamental) who was twice a Roman Catholic and twice a Protestant. Perhaps the song is in fact an 18th-c. up-dating of his remarkable career.

Approached through an attractive 15th-c. gatehouse, **St Michael's Church** dates from the late 13th c. and is predominantly Early English and Perpendicular in style with later restorations of the interior. Inside, notice the medieval brasses and the *Goddard memorial* in the chancel (1620s). William Goddard founded the *Jesus Hospital* almshouse in the village, a charity administered by the Fishmongers' Company of London. Near the village is *Monkey Island* in the Thames, with the former fishing lodge and pavilion of the 3rd Duke of Marlborough (1744), now a hotel and restaurant.

Bulstrode Park see *Gerrards Cross*

Burnham C2
Bucks. Village off A4, in W suburbs of Slough

The site of a 13th-c. abbey whose remains are still to be seen at the modern convent S of the village, Burnham is now part of the 20th-c. sprawl of Slough, though the late medieval and 16th-c. houses which survive are attractive enough. Just off the High Street near the village green stands **St Peter's Church**; founded in the 12th c. and restored in the 1890s, it contains a number of interesting monuments. These include 16th-c. brasses (some of them reused memorials imported from Flanders); a fine bust to a former vicar, John Wright, who died in 1594; black and white marble figures of George Evelyn of Huntercombe and his wife (late 16th-c.) and a white wall monument by the 17th-18th-c. sculptor John Bacon. A pillar on the S arcade of the nave has carved graffiti announcing, among other things, 'the pope is a knave'.

Burnham Beeches C2
Ancient woodlands N of Burnham

Among the rides and walks in the glades and groves are many ancient trees, pollarded in earlier centuries, some more than 300 years old. This has been an admired beauty spot since at least the 1730s when the poet Thomas Gray wrote of the 'venerable beeches'; there are memorials to visits by Mendelssohn and the Swedish soprano Jenny Lind. Covering 600 acres, the place owes its preservation from development to its purchase in the 1880s by the City of London. (See also *Walk 2*, p.18.)

Chalfont St Giles D1
Bucks. Village on A413, 6m NW of Uxbridge.
Event: Chalfont St Giles Show (Sep)

Famous for its association with John Milton, who stayed here with his family during the Great Plague of London (1665-66) the old village is well worth a visit, despite the suburban sprawl that surrounds it. It lies in the valley of the River Misbourne, its old red-brick and timber houses and cottages clustering round a picturesque village green. The old *Rectory* NW of the church is a red and grey brick affair in the classic Queen Anne style, with a hipped roof and a doorcase framed in columns. The little flint **St Giles' Church** is approached through a lych-gate beneath a timber-framed house. Begun in the 12th c. it has a 15th-c. W tower and carved stone entrance. Inside there are a number of 14th-c. wall paintings of the lives of Christ and the Virgin Mary and 15th-c. carved angels in the roof. Monuments include 15th- and 16th-c. brasses in the chancel and the S aisle, and a large wall monument with pediment and black pilasters from the early 1600s. In the churchyard is the grave of Bertram Mills, the circus promoter.

Milton's Cottage (NT) to the SW of the church is now a museum. A modest timber-framed house with a classic cottage garden, it was recommended to the poet as a retreat from the Plague by his friend the Quaker Thomas Ellwood. It was here that Milton finished *Paradise Lost* and began work on *Paradise Regained*.

Down by the river is the old *Mill* and *The Vache*, a 16th-c. manor house standing on a 12th-c. site. Now offices, this was originally the home of the Fleetwood family. Charles Fleetwood married Bridget Ireton, the widowed daughter of Lord Protector Cromwell. The *Park* contains a stately *monument* to Captain Cook, a frequent visitor to the house (he gave its name to a South Sea island).

Hambleden Mill

Above: Henley-on-Thames. Opposite: Hampton Court Palace

In *Newland Park* is the **Chiltern Open Air Museum** of early building, where structures over 500 years old can be seen. There are displays of tools and implements, and there is a *Nature Trail* in the park.

Chalfont St Peter D2
Bucks. Village on A413 (B416), 3m NW of Uxbridge

Though not worth a special visit, the village is interesting for its associations with the 17th-c. pioneers of Quakerism, the Pennington family. The family home was formerly at *The Grange* on the hill above the church, though the present building on the site is a convent school. E of the London Road stands *Chalfont House* in 18th- and 19th-c. 'Gothic'; here the first Lombardy poplars were introduced into England. *St Peter's Church* is an 18th-c. brick Georgian replacement of a medieval original, with 19th-c. Gothic features done by G.E. Street; it has some 15th-c. brasses salvaged from the medieval church. *The Greyhound* is an attractive 17th-c. inn standing by the River Misbourne.

Childe Beale Wildlife Trust see *Goring & Streatley*

Cliveden (NT) C2
Bucks. Historic house on B476 off A5, 8m NW of Windsor

One of the more recent of England's great country houses, Cliveden and its grounds were first laid out on open chalk grasslands overlooking the Thames in the 1660s by the 2nd Duke of Buckingham – Restoration wit and author of *The Rehearsal*. The great arcaded terrace on the S side of the present house was designed by his architect, William Winde, as the platform for a great brick-built mansion. The next owner, George, Earl of Orkney, one of Marlborough's leading generals, made various alterations and added the *Blenheim Pavilion* (1720s) and the *Octagon Temple* (1730s), still to be seen in the grounds. The Earl, advised by his friend the poet Alexander Pope, was also responsible for the basic layout of the formal gardens, notably the parterre on the S side and the yew walks to the W. After the Earl's death, his daughter rented Cliveden to Frederick, Prince of Wales, father of King George III, from 1739-51. It may have been at Cliveden that the young Prince George made his first acquaintance with Lord Bute, a frequent house guest of his father's and an important early influence on the young king, who came to the throne aged 22 in 1760.

In 1795 the great house was destroyed by fire. The next house on the site was built for Sir George Warrender, a noted *bon viveur*, who bought the place in the 1820s. After his death in 1849 it was sold to the 2nd Duke of Sutherland, but this house too was burnt to the ground, as the result of an accident during redecorations. The Duke subsequently employed the architect Sir Charles Barry (designer of the Houses of Parliament) to build the house we see today. Some consider it Barry's masterpiece. He modelled his design on illustrations of the Italianate house as it appeared in the early 1700s. During the tenure of the Sutherlands Queen Victoria was a regular visitor (the Duchess had been Mistress of the Robes at the time of the Queen's coronation) as, also, was Mr Gladstone and leading Liberal politicians. On his visit to England in 1864 the Italian patriot Garibaldi was a house guest.

In 1869 Cliveden changed hands yet again, passing to the Duke of Westminster, son-in-law of the Duchess of Sutherland. Under him, various changes were made. The pillared *porte cochère* was added to the N front, and the interior of the house subjected to alterations. In 1893 Cliveden was bought by the American millionaire William Waldorf Astor, from 1917 1st Viscount Astor. Under him the interior was comprehensively redecorated, the great Renaissance balustrade from Rome's Villa Borghese acquired and re-erected below the S front terrace, and the Long Garden and Water Garden laid out. In 1906 Astor gave

Cliveden: S front

Cliveden to his son Waldorf and his bride Nancy, moving to Hever Castle in Kent.

Now Cliveden moved into its most brilliant period. The vivacious and magnetic Nancy Astor, a perfect foil to her serious-minded husband (who had entered Parliament committed to social reform) presided over house parties which included Henry James, Rudyard Kipling and Winston Churchill among their guests. During World War I Cliveden provided accommodation for the Canadian Military Hospital. On the death of the 1st Viscount Astor in 1919, Waldorf succeeded to the title and was obliged to resign his seat in the Commons. Presenting herself as a candidate at the by-election in her husband's former constituency – Plymouth Devonport – Nancy Astor won a dazzling campaign and was duly elected, becoming the first woman to take her seat as an MP. In the inter-war years the Astors played host to a group of politically radical social leaders, known as the 'Cliveden Set'. In 1942,

the family presented the house to the National Trust, though they continued to live there until the death of the 3rd Lord Astor in 1966. It was then leased by the Trust to Stanford University (California) until 1984, when the lease was taken over by hotel owners. *Cliveden*, the hotel, attempts to recapture the country house atmosphere of Cliveden in its heyday of the '20s and '30s, while part of the interior and all the grounds remain open to the public.

Tour Entering the park by the *Feathers Lodge*, opposite the spacious and comfortable old *Feathers Inn*, the drive leads past the beautiful *Water Garden* (1893-1905) with its island pagoda. From the car park a path leads to the *Fountain of Love*, by the late 19th-c. American sculptor Thomas Waldo Story, which stands at the bottom of the main avenue up to the house. From the centre of the forecourt the N front with its *porte cochère* can be admired, the balustrade along its top echoing that of the main building. The

nine bays of the three-storey façade are divided at second and third floor level by Ionic pilasters. The first floor windows are pedimented, those on the ground floor being arched and framed with rusticated stonework. The balustrade theme is continued along the curving corridors leading to the E and W wings which complete the court. Close to the stable court at the end of the E wing notice the *Clock Tower* (1860s) flanked by its open pillared loggias. Opposite, across the courtyard, are the conservatory and tea-rooms. The forecourt is closed by two yew hedges, along the E of which are a series of eight classical sarcophagi placed here by the 1st Lord Astor.

The *Entrance Hall* is the result of alterations to Barry's design carried out for the 1st Lord Astor by J.L. Pearson. Better known as an architect in the neo-Gothic style, as at Truro Cathedral, Pearson embellished the Hall at Cliveden with designs for oak panelling of classical pilasters and columns topped by a frieze of carved garlands. The French Renaissance stone fireplace was bought by Lord Astor in the 1890s. The *Great Staircase* is to designs by Pearson, and only the painted ceiling survives from Barry's work at Cliveden.

The vast acquisitions by the 1st Lord Astor of furniture, chimneypieces, tapestries and pictures, largely transformed the interior appearance of the house. The panelling and woodcarvings or *boiseries* of the *Dining Room* are French Rococo work created in the mid-18th c. for the Grand Salon of the Chateau d'Asnieres, apparently used primarily as a hunting lodge by the marquis for whom it was built. The ceiling here is a copy of that in the French building. The room retained as the new hotel dining room, overlooking the parterre and the Thames, was originally two drawing rooms. It was made into one great room in the 1870s and later panelled in white and gold by the 1st Lord Astor, who used it as the family drawing room.

Much of the furniture at Cliveden is

18th-c. Italian work, also purchased by Lord Astor; other pieces and some of the fittings, though in the Louis XV style, were made for Cliveden in the 1890s. Among the paintings on show is a portrait of Nancy Astor by Sargent, while other porrtraits include one of the 2nd Duke of Buckingham in the style of Lely and one of the Duchess of Sutherland by the famous Victorian society artist, Winterhalter.

The *Brussels Tapestries* were made for Lord Orkney. Like those carried out later for the Duke of Marlborough at Blenheim, and various other sets by the same workshops for other Marlborough generals, they are based on a series called the 'Arts of War' designed in the 1690s before the victories the English commanders commissioned them to celebrate. The makers were also able to sell other sets of the same designs to allies of Marlborough's French enemies by the simple expedient of changing the titles of the scenes.

Grounds Allow as much time as possible for the visit; the grounds are beautiful and spacious with many features of interest. Leaving the forecourt, turn left along the hedge path to the *Rose Garden*, laid out for the 3rd Lord Astor. Walk on among the trees to the *Ilex Grove*, thought to have been planted in the 1740s (the ilex, or evergreen holm oak, is related to the holly). There is a *bronze* of Prince Albert, no doubt erected because of Queen Victoria's many visits to Cliveden. Next you come to the *Long Garden*, laid out for the 1st Lord Astor (though the flower beds are a later addition) with 18th-c. Italian statues including four figures from the *Commedia dell'Arte*.

Returning to the main path and leaving the Fountain of Love behind you, pass the early 18th-c. *Queen Anne's Vase* to the *Blenheim Pavilion*, with its military trophies in the pediment, put up in the 1720s for Lord Orkney who commanded a brigade in the famous battle. Beyond the pavilion lies the grassy *Amphitheatre*. Here, in August

1740, *Rule Britannia* had its first performance, being one of the arias in Thomas Arne's masque *Alfred* played before Frederick, Prince of Wales. From the Amphitheatre you can make your way down to the banks of the Thames before continuing along the path running parallel to the river to *Canning's Oak*, believed to have been a favourite retreat of the statesman George Canning on his visits to Cliveden in the early 1800s. Certainly, there is a superb vista through the beech trees out along the reach of the Thames. Other equally spectacular views have been re-created by opening up old paths and rides under a National Trust woodland restoration scheme. This entails re-establishing the *Hanging Woods* created by Lord Orkney 280 years ago along a 1½m stretch of the river: replanting will clothe the slopes with cherry, hornbeam, ash, beech and other hardwoods, replacing Lord Orkney's plantation which had suffered badly from Dutch elm disease, gales and drought.

Continuing S with the house away to your left you come to the *Memorial Garden*, commissioned by the 2nd Lord Astor as a cemetery for those who died in the military hospital at Cliveden during World War I. To your left now is the Parterre, but carry on to the *Octagon Temple* with its green copper dome on the edge of the chalk cliffs above the river. The original structure of the 1730s was internally modified in the 1890s to form the Astor family chapel, where many of the family lie buried.

Ahead stretches the Yew Walk (through which you can reach the Boathouse) and the *Spring Drive* sweeping N and W to into the *Russian* (ie. 'Rushy') *Valley*. Otherwise take the path opposite the Octagon for the great *Parterre* formal garden and the view of the S front of the house with the *Borghese Balustrade*. Except for the turfy *Ring*, created for Lord Orkney, the design of the Parterre dates from the 1850s. The *Tortoise Fountain* behind the Ring was made for the 1st

Lord Astor by Thomas Waldo Story. Making for the tearooms round the SE corner of the house you pass the *Duel Sword* turf, cut to commemorate the duel of 1688 between the 2nd Duke of Buckingham and the Earl of Shrewsbury, whose wife was the duke's mistress.

Cookham
C2
Berks. Village on A4094, 3m N of Maidenhead

Famous as the birthplace of the painter Stanley Spencer (1891-1959), the village of Cookham adorns one of the loveliest stretches of the Thames. The iron bridge across the river dates from the 1860s and nearby is a magnificent and comfortable riverside pub. There are many other inns and restaurants in this popular Thames-side resort and a number of handsome houses from the 17th and 18th c. Spencer was not only born here but lived much of his life in the village; the **Stanley Spencer Gallery** at the head of the High Street contains numerous paintings and drawings as well as personal effects of the artist. Also in the High Street (S side) is *Stanley Spencer's Cottage* where the artist was born, and (N side) the attractive 15th-c. *Bel and the Dragon* inn.

Turning towards the river, an old sarsen stone (the *Tarry Stone*) is on the right; once a boundary stone on a different site, this marked the meeting point for village sports in medieval times. **Holy Trinity Church**, on the left, is a Norman foundation which retains the original nave (*c.* 1140), though the tower is 15th-c. There are a number of good monuments, including many medieval brasses and a beautiful early 19th-c. sculptured relief to Isaac Pocock by John Flaxman (1810). A friend of William Blake, Flaxman became the first professor of sculpture at the Royal Academy.

Beyond *Cookham Bridge*, featured in Spencer's paintings, is *Turks Boatyard* with the house of the Queen's Swankeeper, who in July dons his ancient costume to supervise the ceremony of Swan Upping, the counting of the swans.

A pleasant walk can be taken by the towpath (approached from the car park W of the village) along the river to *Winter Hill* (NT) 3m W. This vantage point offers a splendid panorama of the river, as far as Bourne End to the E and Marlow to the W. On nearby *Cock Marsh* (NT) are the **Round Barrows**, which date from Bronze Age and Saxon times. (See *Walk 6*, p.19.)

Dorney   C2
Bucks. Village on B3026, 1½m W of Eton

Dorney Court, the great house by the church, has been the home of the Palmer family since the 1620s. Its Tudor appearance is much indebted to later additions, to the original late 15th-c. building. Norman in origin, **St James's Church** has Tudor brickwork mingling with the clunch and flint of the original 12th-c. structure. The Norman font is still to be seen. There is a 16th-c. chapel to the Garrard family, the Palmers' predecessors here, and the nave with its 18th-c. box pews and 1630s timber musicians' gallery recalls the days of England's patriarchal squirearchy. The decorations include traces of 15th-c. wall paintings, but the great ornament of St James's will be found in the *Garrard Chapel* where stands the large early 16th-c. wall monument to Sir William Garrard, sometime Lord Mayor of London. Two arched niches between three black Corinthian columns contain the large kneeling figures of the knight in dress armour and his consort in black gown and hood. Skulls are to be seen peering from roundels on either side. Below the parents and a pair of black memorial tablets framed by cherubs, their seven sons and eight daughters, some carrying skulls, kneel in prayer – their coat of arms forming a frieze above their heads.

Charles II was a frequent visitor to **Dorney Court**, home of his favourite, Barbara Villiers. In 1668 the King was the gracious recipient of the first pineapple grown in England, raised by Dorney's gardener Charles Rose. A reproduction of Danckerts' painting

commemorating the event hangs in the great house, and *The Pineapple Inn* was later named in its honour. The *Gardens* with their flower beds and yew hedges make a pleasant setting.

Dorneywood (NT)   C2
Bucks. Mansion and estate off A355, 7m N of Windsor

The winding road on the southern outskirts of Burnham Beeches passes the entrance to this stately home of the 20th c. Built in 1920, it was presented to the National Trust in 1942 by the owner, Lord Courtauld-Thomson, to serve as an official residence for either a Secretary of State or a Minister of the Crown. Only the **Grounds** of the 200-acre estate are open to the public (Saturday afternoons in August and September) and written application should be made to the Secretary of the Dorneywood Trust.

Much of the house can be seen from the road, as can the splendid brick and timber-frame Tudor barn and farmhouse which now accommodates the domestic staff. From Windsor, the best way to approach Dorneywood is to drive to Burnham and take the right hand fork just N of the village where Dorneywood is sign-posted.

Eton   C3
Berks. Town on A308 (A332), ½m N of Windsor.
Event: College Founder's Day (Jun). EC Wed. Inf:
Tel (95) 52010

Eton is best reached on foot from Windsor. The iron bridge (1824) over the Thames is closed to traffic, but approached on foot down Thames Street and Lower Thames Street in Windsor it gives quick access to Eton High Street. This offers a pleasant stroll past antique shops and cafés such as *The Eton Buttery* to Eton College.

Eton College England's most famous school was founded in 1440 by King Henry VI as 'The King's College of Our Lady of Eton beside Windsor'. The foundation, lavishly endowed with land revenues and holy relics, envisaged an establishment of 10 priests, 10 chaplains, 10 clerks and 16 choristers for the service of the chapels, and 70 king's scholars. There was to be a great pilgrimage church, planned as one of the largest in the kingdom.

The Lower School building, with a large single classroom (still in daily use) below, and a dormitory (the Long Chamber, now divided into separate study bedrooms for scholars) above, was completed in 1443 and the College Hall about a decade later. Accommodation was provided for priests and fellows around Cloister Court, and by 1460 the chancel of the great church was nearing completion. The following year, however, Henry VI of the House of Lancaster was deposed and the Yorkist King Edward IV came to the throne. Most of Eton's endowments were transferred to Windsor and the new school seemed in danger. King Edward relented – under persuasion, it is said, from his mistress Jane Shore. In the 1470s the chancel was roofed in timber and, despite much reduced revenues, the school continued. But in place of the great nave which had been planned, the chancel was closed off (1482) with the building of the antechapel.

The fortunes of the College improved when Henry VII, who claimed descent from the Lancastrians, usurped the throne in 1485. Buildings known as Lupton's Range were completed along the E side of School Yard by 1520. In the late 17th c. a second large classroom, Upper School, was built along the W side of the School Yard.

From the beginning there were provisions for the education of boys from the town ('Oppidans') alongside the king's scholars so that, although a private foundation, Eton was also a 'public' school. From the 17th c. the ranks of the Oppidans were swelled by the sons of the nobility as the royal foundation became increasingly fashionable. They lived in houses in the town and today's 24 boarding houses developed from this system. The 70 scholars were heavily outnumbered by the wealthy Oppidans, and by the 1760s the school population had risen to more than 500 pupils. Classes in the two huge rooms could number as many as 200 boys and discipline, such as it was, was maintained by corporal punishment. Masters attempting to inculcate the rudiments of Greek and Latin were regularly pelted with missiles ranging from bad eggs to books. Today there are some 1200 boys and the educational facilities at the College are outstanding.

In games, as in everything else, Eton has its own traditions. Eton Fives developed from a ball game played between the buttresses by the stairs outside the Chapel. The Eton Wall Game, an annual contest between the College and Oppidans, remains a mystery to all but Etonians. The Eton Field Game is a kind of soccer which also incorporates a scrum, as in rugger. The Eton Boat Club claims to be the world's largest, and the Eton Boating Song is accepted as part of England's nostalgic heritage. Eton has its own school slang, and its own school dress in which tail suits and wing collars feature and are retained by majority vote of the boys.

Tour The college is approached by the Long Walk, which can be reached either from Eton High Street or Slough Road. On the W side are the *Memorial Buildings* of *School Hall* (1908) and the octagonal *School Library*, and to the E the Upper School and the buttressses of the antechapel. The entrance to the *School Yard* is in the centre of the Upper School building.

At the centre of School Yard stands the early 18th-c. *statue* of Henry VI in Garter robes. Behind you are the arcades of Upper School; ahead the fine Lupton's Tower with its clock and pinnacles and, to the left, Lower School. To the right is the College Chapel, set well above ground level as a precaution against flooding. By the stairs of its N door, between the buttresses of its N wall, is the space used as the original Eton fives court.

On the right, at the end of the Upper School buildings, is the late 15th-c. wooden door to the stairs of the

Antechapel (1479-82), built by Eton's second great benefactor. Bishop Wayneflete. The W wall of the antechapel is lined with panelling and bronze memorial plaques to former members of the college; a group of 15th- and 16th-c. brasses are mounted on the wall to the right of the screen entrance to the chapel proper. The magnificent heraldic tablets on the N and S walks of the antechapel and the windows above them are memorials to old Etonians who died in the Crimean War.

College Chapel Created from the chancel of Henry VI's projected church, the Chapel stands as a fine example of 15th-c. Perpendicular. Its greatest treasure is the series of *wall paintings* depicting the miracles of the Virgin Mary and other saints. Done in the grisaille technique of grey and sepia tones in the late 15th c. by William Baker, they are among the finest examples of English medieval art. Whitewashed over in the 1560s, in conformity with Protestant theology, they were uncovered during 19th-c. restoration work. However, the upper scenes had been scraped off with the whitewash and the lower scenes covered again with choir stall canopies – this time in conformity with Victorian taste. The paintings were re-exposed in the 1920s and restoration work begun in the early 1960s was finally completed in 1975. The fan vaulting of the Chapel roof is made of stone-faced concrete hung from a steel frame, and was put up in the 1950s to replace the decayed timbers of the 15th-c. original. The glass in the *E window* by Evie Hone was installed in 1952 to replace the window shattered by bombing during 1940. It depicts the Crucifixion above and the Last Supper below, with deep vibrant colours in the classic tradition of medieval stained glass. The windows to either side of the chancel were made to designs by John Piper; those on the N side depict four of Christ's miracles, those on the S side four of his parables. Against the N wall before the altar steps is a late 18th-c. German-built chamber organ. The small *Chapel* behind this is dedicated to Old Etonians who fell in the World Wars; to the E is the somewhat larger *Lupton Chapel* (1515) with a lovely gilded fan-vaulted ceiling.

From the Chapel cross School Yard to **Lupton's Tower**. This was built in 1520 by Henry Redman, who also worked on Hampton Court Palace. The corner turrets are topped with 17th-c. timber lanterns; in the niche between the two oriel windows is a medieval statue of the Virgin Mary.

Lupton's Tower, Eton College

The arch under the tower leads to the *Cloisters*. The two lower storeys of this court date from the 1440s, the upper storey being added in the mid-18th c. Above the S colonnade is the *Old Library* (closed to visitors), an elegant 18th-c. interior of galleried rooms, delicate plasterwork, handsome bookcases and busts of Old Etonians. Its treasures include medieval deeds, three books printed by Caxton and a Gutenberg Bible (*c* 1455), one of the world's six oldest books printed with moveable type. On view to the public, in the undercroft beneath College Hall, is the **Museum of Eton Life** which opened in 1985. Here can be seen displays of College history, curricula, uniforms and other items.

Near the old pump in the *S cloister* a flight of stone steps leads up to the *College Hall* with its fine timber roof, completed *c.* 1450. A passage in the NE corner of the cloisters leads to *College Field* and the long wall against which is played the Wall Game. Returning to School Yard enter **Lower School**, opposite the Chapel. Completed in the 1440s, it is thought to be the world's oldest classroom in continual use. Its long desks and benches are liberally carved with the names of old boys, the earliest dating from the 1550s; timber arches marching the length of the room support the beams of the *Long Chamber* dormitory above. The old *Brewhouse*, approached from School Yard between the Chapel and Lupton's Range, dates from the early 18th c.; it is now an art gallery.

Upper School, built in the late 17th c., houses the *Long Room* lined with busts of famous old boys, notably the Duke of Wellington, Mr Gladstone, the poets Thomas Gray and Shelley and Lord North, prime minister at the time of the loss of the American colonies. At the end of the room is the cubicle with the desk of Dr Keate, the school's notorious headmaster who once thrashed more than 100 boys following a school rebellion in 1832. The screwholes where the boys barred him in can still be seen.

Fawley B1
Bucks. Village off B480, 2½m N of Henley

Another charming Chilterns village on wooded slopes, with cottages and farms stretching along its ridge overlooking the Thames Valley. **St Mary's Church**, established in the 13th c., retains its original tower but was much restored in the mid-18th c. and again in the 19th c. Notice the carved 17th-c. pulpit and the marbled monument to Justice Sir James Whitelock (1630s), and church furnishings brought from Canons, the house of the dukes of Chandos near Edgware. The churchyard has two interesting old *mausoleums*.

¾m to the SE of the village stands *Fawley Court*, a mansion of the 1680s in the style of, though probably not by, Sir Christopher Wren. Today it is a private school. The classical colonnade was added *c.* 1800 by James Wyatt. The interiors include Adam-style decoration and some splendid late 17th-c. plasterwork and fireplaces.

Fingest B1
Bucks. Village off B482, 5m SW of High Wycombe

Set in a wooded Chiltern hollow, the old cottages and splendid brick pub *The Chequers* are dwarfed by the remarkable tower of **St Bartholomew's Church**. A massive 60-ft high Norman structure of flint, with walls more than 3ft thick, it has handsome round-arched bell openings near the roof line and is topped, unusually, by a tiled double-gable roof. The narrow and diminutive nave is quite out of proportion with the fortress-like tower.

From the T junction opposite the pub, a public footpath leads through the woods and across fields to **Turville* 1½m W (see *Walk 4*, p.18).

Fulmer C2
Bucks. Village off B416, 4m N of Slough

Georgian and neo-Georgian houses are a feature of this village in a hollow of the Chilterns S of Gerrards Cross. **St James's Church** is an early 17th-c. re-building of the original medieval structure, done in mellow red brick; it was subject to heavy restoration work in the 1870s by G.E. Street. The monument to Sir Marmaduke Dayrell (d. 1631) beneath its pillared canopy shows the knight in armour, his lady at his side in a black dress; beneath them kneel their two sons and their families.

Gerrards Cross D2
Bucks. On A40/B416, 9m N of Windsor

A commuter suburb which began to flourish around the rail station of the old Great Central Line in the last century and has continued to grow in the age of the car. Victorian villas and opulent if unremarkable 20th-c. homes and apartment blocks spread out from the wooded common on the A40. On the W edge is the large and splendid *Bull Hotel*; once an important coaching inn, it received its handsome white frontage in the early 19th c. *St James's Church* (1860s) designed by Sir William Tite, is an exotic mélange of Romanesque arches, Italianate and pagoda-roofed towers and a lead Byzantine-like dome tricked out with Gothic pediments. To the W along the A40 is *Bulstrode Park*, an 1860s mansion set in parkland landscaped by Humphry Repton for an earlier house. The estate dates back to pre-Conquest times, the former house providing a residence for Judge Jeffreys from 1676 till his death in 1689, and a meeting place for many important politicians and intellectuals under the aegis of the 2nd Duchess of Portland in the 18th c. There is a small Iron Age *hill fort* with double ramparts in the park.

Goring and Streatley A2
Oxon & Berks. Twin towns on B4009 (A329), 17m NW of Reading

Since Edwardian times Goring has been one of the more fashionable Thames-side towns, but many consider Streatley, across the attractive wooden bridge, the prettier of the two. At the western limit of our territory, they nestle in the valley of the river as it wends its way between the wooded Chiltern Hills and the Berkshire Downs through the Goring Gap, a place of some strategic importance in

the calculations of England's medieval kings. The view from the bridge, with upstream the lock and the weir and river cruisers of varying opulence lined along the banks, is a comfortable idyll. Gabled boathouses and the balconies of wealthy residences overlook the river. **Goring's** 12th-c. **Church of St Thomas of Canterbury** has an impressive nave arch and 15th- and 17th-c. brasses. Goring Priory was among the many of England's medieval glories destroyed in Henry VIII's Dissolution of the Monasteries, but *Elvendon Priory*, 1½m W of the town, probably incorporates a medieval hall house that once belonged to the nuns.

Little more than a village, **Streatley** is a place of charming cottages and Georgian town houses and has a gabled 19th-c. *Malt-house*. The bushy chalk bluff of *Streatley Hill* gives a vantage point for views over the hills of the Goring Gap to the meadows by the Thames and the National Trust properties of Larden Chase and Lough Down.

Another National Trust property nearby is **Basildon Park**, 2m S along the A329. Built in the 1770s, it stands on a hill amidst park and woodland. The house has some beautiful interiors adorned with fine plasterwork; there is an impressive octagon room and many outstanding pictures and pieces of furniture. There are good views over the Thames valley from the surrounding parkland.

A little further on in Lower Basildon, by Church Farm, the **Childe Beale Wildlife Trust** nature reserve and bird sanctuary are open to visitors throughout the summer.

Hambleden B2
Bucks. Village off A4155, 3m NE of Henley-on-Thames

Approaching along the A4155 Henley-Marlow road in the Hambleden Valley, you turn off for Hambleden at *Mill End*. Here the large white bulk of the weatherboarded *Hambleden Mill* and the timber *Mill House* stand near the road. The great zig-zag weir across the river offers an exciting causeway walk to Hambleden Lock. (See also *Walk 3* p.18.) The scene is picturesque but the road, between brick-built cottages, is narrow and hazardous. There is a convenient car park.

1m N among the wooded beech slopes, under National Trust protection, lies Hambleden village, with its 17th-c. *Manor House* and Georgian houses grouped around the green. An 11th-c. foundation, **St Mary's Church** has been greatly altered by restoration and rebuilding over the centuries, so that its picturesque tower now looks something like an 18th-c. Gothick folly. The churchyard, entered by a lychgate, contains an interesting 18th-c. domed mausoleum among its monuments, and within the church is a handsome alabaster monument to Sir Cope d'Oyley (1630s) with wife and kneeling children in attendance.

Hampton Court Palace   D4
Greater London. Historic building off A308

A ˉroyal residence from the days of Henry VIII to Queen Victoria, Hampton Court began as a palace built in 1514 by Thomas Wolsey, who became Archbishop of York the same year. The following year he was created Cardinal by Pope Clement VII and appointed Lord Chancellor by Henry. In 1525, in a princely gesture to his royal master, Wolsey accepted a royal house at Richmond in exchange for his palace. Wolsey died in disgrace, nevertheless, in 1530.

Henry was impressed by the palace and ordered substantial enlargements and alterations. He was always impatient, and work on the Great Hall was pressed on even at night in the glow of a thousand candles. In addition the king enlarged the Chapel Royal and built state apartments. He also laid out fine formal gardens and for his sport a deer park, a tilt-yard and a Real Tennis court (still the home of the game).

The palace, which under Henry had been the magnificent setting of his opulent court, became a favourite retreat for his children: Edward VI, Mary I and Elizabeth. It continued in favour under the first Stuart kings and was used by Lord Protector Cromwell. During the brief reign of James II it fell into neglect, but the year after his fall in 1688 the joint monarchs William III and Mary II commissioned Sir Christopher Wren to plan a new palace here that was to outshine Versailles. Wren's first designs, lively and vigorous, were rejected possibly because, according to one art historian, they failed to capture 'the regal monotony of the Park Front at Versailles'. More restrained designs, gracefully classical in style, were prepared, but in the event shortage of funds meant that only part of these could be fulfilled.

Wren had to plan two sets of state rooms, one set each for the joint monarchs. The Tudor buildings of the old Cloister Green Court were pulled down. The new royal apartments formed the wings on the E and S sides of what is now the Fountain Court. The old Tudor formal gardens were swept away and replaced by the Great Fountain Garden, the Broad Walk, the Wilderness and the Maze. The Chestnut Avenue towards Bushy Park was laid out as the grand approach to the new Versailles.

In the 1720s, Sir John Vanbrugh refurbished a suite in the NE corner of the palace for George II's eldest son Frederick, Prince of Wales, and a decade later William Kent built the Cumberland Suite for George, Duke of Cumberland, the king's second son. But Hampton Court's days as a royal palace were numbered: George III never resided here and early in Victoria's reign the buildings were opened to the public.

Tour The entrance is over the moat flanked by royal beasts and through the *Great Gatehouse* (rebuilt by George II). This leads into the *Base Court* with its Tudor chambers. Facing is the Tudor *Clock Gatehouse*, also known as *Anne Boleyn's Gateway*, with towers embellished with terracotta medallions of Roman emperors by Giovanni Maiano, and the arms of Thomas Wolsey over the entrance. Passing through the gatehouse into the *Clock Court*, the inner front is topped by an astronomical clock built for Henry VIII by Nicolas Oursian.

On the SE side of Clock Court is the entrance to Wren's State Apartments. They are reached by the *King's Staircase*, adorned with ceiling paintings by Antonio Verrio (1700), via the *King's Guardroom* with its armoury collection, to the *King's Apartments*. The sequence of rooms is from the most public (The King's First Presence Chamber) to the most private (Bedroom, Dressing Room and Writing Closet). Parallel to the King's Apartments, overlooking the Fountain Court, is the *Cartoon Gallery* built by Wren to house the Raphael Cartoons, one of the great art treasures of Charles I (these are tapestry copies; the originals are in the Victoria and Albert Museum, London). From the King's Apartments proceed through the E and N sides of the court, containing the *Queen's Gallery and Apartments* and a range of private chambers built for George II in 1732.

Beyond the Queen's Apartments is the **Chapel Royal** built by Wolsey and enlarged by Henry VIII, who built the King's Pew. Behind this runs the gallery supposed to be haunted by Catherine Howard, the king's fifth wife. Under house arrest in the palace for suspected adultery, she tried to reach the king to beg for mercy. She was dragged back by the soldiers and subsequently executed for treason on Tower Green in London (1542).

Nearby is *Wolsey's Closet*, the only remaining room furnished in the style of the Cardinal's house. It has linenfold panelling on the lower part of the walls with panels of New Testament scenes above. The ceiling has Renaissance plasterwork with Tudor roses. The main surviving part of Henry's palace consists of the *Great Watching Chamber* and **Great Hall**, where he held masques and feasts. The magnificent hammerbeam roof is decorated with painted ornaments, including Anne Boleyn's initials and falcon device dating it to 1533-36. Also in this section of the palace are the *Great Tudor Kitchens*.

Also worth visiting is the **Orangery**, housing the paintings *The Triumphs of Caesar* by Mantegna (1485-95). Special features of the **Gardens**, open to the public, are the Maze, Wilderness, Privy Garden and Pond Garden. The *Great Vine*, planted in 1768, still bears fruit.

Hell Fire Caves see *West Wycombe*

Henley-on-Thames   B2
Oxon. Pop 11,860. 13m NW of Windsor (A423/A4155/A321). Events: Henley Royal Regatta (late Jun-early Jul); Henley Town Regatta (last Sat in Jul or 1st Sat in Aug). EC Wed MD Thur. Inf: Tel (0491) 578034

The world-famous Henley Royal Regatta, held annually on the Straight Mile in late June/early July, originated from a regatta first held in 1839 to boost the town's commerce – a pioneering instance of tourist promotion. Ten years earlier Henley had witnessed the first Oxford-Cambridge University Boat Race. There was a river settlement here at least as early as the 12th c. which developed into a port trading timber, corn and malt to London. A group of timber-framed cottages to be seen on Thames Side were originally a 15th-c. granary. During the 18th c. Henley was an important coaching town and it is still noted for its fine hotels and ancient inns, as well as being the centre for a number of quality antique shops. Nearby are the great houses of *Stonor Park and *Rotherfield Greys.

Approaching on the A423 from Windsor or the A321 from Twyford you pass the Leander Club headquarters for the Regatta and the 16th-c. *Little Angel* inn and enter the town over *Henley Bridge*. The heads representing the Thames and Isis (the name for the Thames when it runs through Oxford) over the central arches were done at the rebuilding of the bridge in the 1780s. Looking towards the town you see *The Angel on the Bridge Inn* (left) and *The*

Red Lion (right) and, rising behind them, the Tudor tower of St Mary's Church. One of the cellars of the 17th-c. *Angel Inn* encloses an arch of the medieval bridge and its riverside terrace is a favourite haunt at regatta time. The 17th-c. *Red Lion*, once Henley's main coaching inn, was rebuilt in red brick in the 18th c. Charles I and Rupert of the Rhine stayed at the original hostelry during the Civil War, while Boswell and Johnson dined in the present building in the 1770s. The Prince Regent is reputed to have consumed 14 of the landlady's renowned lamb cutlets at a single sitting, and Wellington and Blücher lodged here after Waterloo. The recommended tour of the town starts from the King's Road car park; you reach it by driving up Hart Street from the Bridge (straight on) to Market Place and right at the Town Hall into King's Road.

Tour Walk back down King's Road to the junction with West Street; on the corner (No 4) is the early 18th-c. *West Hill House*, with handsome doorcase and roof remodelled in the 1830s. Opposite is the early-1900s Queen Anne-style *Town Hall*, which houses the Information Centre in the basement. To the left is the Market Place, to the right Gravel Hill with pretty Georgian cottages and then the dramatic Gothic Victorian lodge to *Friar Park*, a highly eccentric 1890s mansion. Opposite the lodge there is a pretty 16th-c. *Cottage*.

The *Market Place* (Thursday Market) is lined with picturesque 16th-18th-c. buildings; a left turn into the main shopping street, Bell Street, opens another vista. *No 16*, with its central carriageway arch, was built in the late 18th c. as the Assembly Rooms. *The Bull Inn* dates from the 15th c. and *The Bear Inn* from the 16th c. – originally their inn-yards were the scene of bull and bear baiting. Turn right by a 16th-c. house with a projecting upper storey down New Street. Here are: *Saragossa House* (*c.* 1700); the **Kenton Theatre** (1805) which

seats 250 and is one of England's earliest surviving theatre buildings; the 15th-c. *Anne Boleyn* and *Tudor Cottages*, timber-framed and with projecting upper storeys; Brakspear's *Henley Brewery* (1890s) and *Malthouses* (also 1890s) with their timber drying towers; and the imposing *Old Brewery House* of the 1730s. Turn right at Riverside along a pretty row of Victorian boathouses past the pretty, late 19th-c. *Little White Hart Hotel* and the pedimented arched gateway to the stable of *The Red Lion*, with distant glimpses of wooded hills across the Thames. This lovely walk continues beyond the bridge as Thames Side to the mediaeval *'Granary' cottages* at the corner of Friday Street. Across the bridge another good walking route follows the towpath N to Hambleden Lock (see *Walk 3*, p.18).

Return along Thames Side to the Bridge and turn left up Hart Street to **St Mary's Church**, much restored in the 19th c. The interior dates from the 13th c., though *St Leonard's Chapel* is 15th-c. The church contains a 17th-c. Flemish painting of the Virgin; a notable 1620s alabaster and black marble monument and a wealth of Victorian stained glass, including the rich E window in the N chapel (1860s). NE of the church is the early 15th-c. timber-framed *Chantry House* and, on the W side of the churchyard, the *Almshouses*, founded in the 1530s and rebuilt in the 1830s. Continue up Hart Street with its 15th-18th-c. houses to Market Place, the Town Hall and so to the car park.

The magnificent mansion of **Stonor Park* is a short excursion from Henley. Take the A423 N: leaving the town notice the majestic old *Town Houses* along North Field End and Fair Mile.

High Wycombe C1

Bucks. Pop 60,516 17m NW of Windsor (M40/A40/A4128/A404). EC Wed, MD Fri. Inf: Tel (0494) 26100

For two centuries the traditional centre of the furniture industry, High Wycombe, stretching along the valley of the River Wye, has been a settlement at least since Roman times.

During the Middle Ages it was a major wool centre and later became known for its lace. It was in the 17th c., when growing national prosperity and the development of household economies began to produce a mass market for furniture, that High Wycombe really began to exploit its great natural resource – the beechwoods surrounding the town. These began to be dotted with the huts and cottages of 'chair bodgers' – cottage craftsmen turning out chair legs and rails by the gross for assembly in Wycombe itself and for export to assembly factories in Birmingham or London. During the 18th c. Wycombe was an important coaching town and its furniture industry began to grow considerably – according to tradition it was a Wycombe manufacturer who produced the high-backed armchair which won the approval of King George III and became known as the 'Windsor' chair. Modern industries include paper manufacture and engineering, printing works and pharmaceuticals.

Although the M40 relieves the centre of much through traffic it can still be very congested, but approaching from the E the visitor can enjoy the long stretch of the *Rye*, 30 acres of parkland along the little river. The large *Town Hall* in Queen Victoria Road, in late Renaissance style, was built in the early 1900s, but something of the feel of historic Wycombe survives at the end of High Street. Here the handsome mid-18th-c. *Guildhall* comprises a brick upper storey supported on elegant arches and classical columns. Opposite stands the *Little Market House* or *Shambles*, an unusual octagonal structure built to designs by Robert Adam in 1761. Both were built with funds provided by the local magnate Lord Shelbourne. A number of other attractive old buildings have survived the planner's blight which has afflicted much of the town, notably *The Falcon Inn* and *The Antelope*. Of *The Red Lion* in High Street only the façade survives, despite the fact that it was from here that both Disraeli and Chur-

chill addressed the electors of Wycombe. The **Wycombe Chair & Local History Museum** on Castle Hill has many fine examples of craftsmen's work, including chairs from the early 17th c. to the time of Chippendale, Hepplewhite and Sheraton.

Norman in origin, the **Church of St Nicholas** is a basically 13th-c. structure, though the upper stage of the tower was added in the 1750s and the general air of the building derives from two large schemes of Victorian restoration. The church has the only 12-bell ring in the county of Buckingham, and contains many interesting monuments, including one to famous women of history which was erected in the 1930s.

Hughenden
C1
Bucks. Village off A4128, 1½m N of High Wycombe

The manor house (see below), home of Benjamin Disraeli, Lord Beaconsfield, is the chief attraction here, but the little village **Church** among the trees at the bottom of the park should be visited; nearby is a range of 17th-c. gabled *Almshouses*. In the churchyard notice the venerable square-cut *yew tree* planted in 1690, and the *Disraeli tomb* where lie the bodies not only of the prime minister but also of his wife, his brother James, and Sarah Williams, long time Benjamin's friend, who bequeathed him a fortune and willed that she might share his grave. The font, chancel and de Montfort side chapel survive from the medieval period, but otherwise the church is largely the result of 19th-c. restoration work. The *de Montfort Chapel* receives its name from the fact that the Wellesbourne family – lords of the manor here in the 16th c. – claimed (spuriously) descent from the 13th-c. champion of parliament, Simon de Montfort. The capitals of an arcade linking the chapel and nave bear heraldic shields which ingeniously combine the Wellesbourne and de Montfort arms. Of the six intriguing memorial effigies, five have been said to be 16th-c. copies, suitably altered for the Wellesbournes, of earlier medieval carvings. The sixth, also 16th-c., is of a corpse in a shroud – the liberated soul carved in its hollow chest.

Hughenden Manor (NT) The house was bought by Disraeli in 1847, and was his home until his death in 1881. During this period the original Georgian stucco mansion was much altered, receiving an ornamental parapet balustrade and a heavily remodelled exterior, while within there is Gothic-and Tudor-style vaulting, panelling and moulding. Disraeli's superb library, furniture and pictures are preserved, and the study is kept as it was at the time of Disraeli's death. The **Disraeli Museum** contains collections of his letters and other memorabilia.

The house has an attractive Italian-style terraced *Garden* and is surrounded by wooded parkland.

Hurley B2
Berks. Village off A423 (A404), 5m NW of Maidenhead

The Thames here splits into a number of channels, to cause backwaters and islands and the kind of riverscape that must have existed before the introduction of weirs and locks made in the 18th and 19th c. *Ye Olde Bell Inn* at Hurley, claimed as one of the oldest in England, was the unofficial HQ of General Eisenhower before the Normandy landings of World War II, and has many mementoes of the period.

According to tradition Edith, sister of King Edward the Confessor, was buried in the village's Anglo-Saxon church, and shortly after the Norman Conquest a Benedictine monastery was founded here. The parish **Church**, essentially a Norman structure, has remnants of Anglo-Saxon work and was heavily restored in the 19th c. It incorporates part of the church of the monastery here, which was dissolved at the time of the Reformation. The **Monastery** buildings, ruins of which can be seen in the *'Paradise' Quadrangle*, passed to the Lovelace family, whose monuments are in the church.

Iver D3
Bucks. Village on B470, 3m E of Slough

A pretty place with a number of great houses in the surrounding countryside and, a few miles to the N, *Iver Heath* and the Pinewood film studios. **St Peter's Church**, with its 13th-c. battlemented tower, is an Anglo-Saxon foundation. Much of the original nave survives, the aisles being 12th-15th-c.

Of special beauty is the 12th-c. chancel, with its wide pointed arch. There is a Norman font and a pretty 17th-c. pulpit carved with cherubs. Among the brasses and monuments, the most dramatic is that of Lady Mary Salter (d. 1631) depicted half-rising from a black coffin, surrounded by columns and adorned with cherubs.

Opposite the church, across the village green, is the old timber-framed *Swan Inn*, and down by the river the early 18th-c. *Bridgefoot House* in yellow brick behind its wrought-iron gates. On the road towards Iver Heath lies the early 19th-c. yellow-brick *Iver Lodge* and, down Coppins Lane, the royal residence of *Coppins*. A Victorian building, it was bought by Princess Victoria early in the 20th c. and is especially associated with the family of the dukes of Kent.

Iver Heath D2
Bucks. Village on A412, 4m NE of Slough

An undistinguished village with interesting associations. Amid the pine woods between it and the M40, the Georgian mansion of Heatherden Hall was, in the early 1900s, the home of the great cricketer Ranjitsinhji. From him it passed to the Morden family, and in the study was ratified the Irish Free State Treaty of 1921. Then, in the 1930s, the house and 100 acres of estates was bought by Charles Boot, a rich man with the ambition to establish a British Hollywood-type film industry. The **Pinewood Studios** were opened in September 1936 with J. Arthur Rank as chairman. The old house and its beautiful gardens became the focus for scores of studio stages and outside sets. Herbert Wilcox was the first director to work on the site; Carol Reed the first to shoot a complete film here. During World War II the Crown Film Unit produced morale-boosting propaganda features and outstanding documentaries under the brilliant director Humphrey Jennings. After the war it became part of the Rank Organization and one of Europe's largest and best equipped film studios. In recent years Pinewood's world-beating box office successes have included the Superman films and the James Bond films. The motorist may catch glimpses of film sets from the road, but unfortunately the busy studios do not have time to offer tours to the public.

Jordans
Bucks. Village between A40 (Beaconsfield) & A413 (Chalfont St Giles)
D1

Nestling among the wooded slopes of the Chilterns, Jordans is a delightful centre for the rambler. It is also a place of pilgrimage, for here lies buried William Penn (d. 1718), the founder of Pennsylvania and a leading member of the early Quakers. Penn and two of his wives are just three of the numerous founder members of the Society of Friends buried in the lawns around the handsome brick **Friends' Meeting House** at Jordans, built in 1687. The furnishings are simple and austere, and the walls are hung with portraits and other mementos of early Friends. Before the Meeting House was built, following the Declaration of Indulgence by the Catholic King James II which promulgated toleration of religious groups outside the Church of England, the Quakers hereabouts had held their meetings at *Old Jordans Farm*, now a hostel. The farm's **Mayflower Barn** is so called because its roof timbers are traditionally supposed to have come from the ship of that name. The barn is open to view.

Lacey Green
Bucks. Village off A4010, 3m N of High Wycombe
C1

The large **Smock Mill**, built some time in the middle of the 17th c., was moved here in 1821. It is a fine example of the type, thanks to the Chiltern Society

which completed a 6-year restoration programme in 1978.

The pubs hereabouts have interesting associations. The ancient *Plow* at the neighbouring village of *Speen* was once run by Ishbel MacDonald, daughter of the Labour Prime Minsister Ramsay MacDonald, while *The Pink and Lily* in Lacey Green itself was a favourite haunt of Rupert Brooke in the 1910s. To reach it you take the little road to the N out of the village passing '*Wardrobes*' where a house of this name has stood since the 14th c. (It is thought the original was built for a retired clerk of the Wardrobe, one of the great medieval offices of state.) The pub supposedly derives its name from a Mr Pink, a butler, and Lily, the parlourmaid he married in the early 1800s. The bar parlour proudly displays a verse dashed off by Brooke on a visit:

Never came there to the Pink
Two such men as we, I think.
Never came here to the Lily
Two men quite so richly silly.

Langley Marish
Berks. Village on B470, in E suburbs of Slough
C3/D3

Usually known simply as Langley, the village boasts a treasure quite unexpected in the uninspiring built-up area of Slough: the **Church of Mary the Virgin**. Flanked by the ranges of two 17th-c. *Almshouses* founded by the Kederminster family and the Seymours (to the N) the church was founded in the 12th c. and is a mixture of many styles. The battlemented brick tower dates from the early 1600s, and the *Kederminster Chapel* with painted and lattice panels – 'little more than a large family pew' – is also of the 17th c.

Beyond the chapel is one of the region's most remarkable interiors. This is the **Kederminster Library**, said to have been used by John Milton when he was staying at nearby Horton. Built on to the S door in 1623, the room is lined with more than 200 painted decorative panels, views of Windsor Castle and other local landscapes; there is also a handsome and elaborate chimneypiece. Many of the finest books of Sir John Kederminster's 17th-c. private library are now housed in the British Museum in London, among them the 12th-c. 'Kederminster Gospels', but a fascinating volume of herbal remedies used by Sir John and his wife is still here, together with scores of other fine old books. The library with its well-preserved original paintwork and recently-refurbished books can be visited by arrangement.

Maidenhead
C2

Berks. Pop 49,038. 7m NW of Windsor (A308/A4). Event: Maidenhead Regatta (Aug). EC Thur MD Fri, Sat. Inf: Tel (0628) 25657

For the most part a pleasant residential town, Maidenhead can boast no special architectural interest except for the railway viaduct on the outskirts, known as the **Sounding Arch** because of its echo and built in 1838 by Brunel; this was the viaduct in Turner's famous painting *Rain, Steam and Speed*. Maidenhead's **Henry Reitlinger Bequest Museum** in Guards Club Road has an interesting collection of glass, ceramics, sculpture and paintings. Down by the river you can see the beautifully restored barge of Jesus College, Oxford, brought here by a recent benefactor and a glorious reminder of the leisured splendour of summer life on the Thames of earlier days.

The river has been central to Maidenhead's history since the 13th c. when the first bridge was built here – the present bridge dates from the 18th c. At this time the little town was an important coaching centre with scores of inns. Today, the oldest building is the 1659 *Smith's Almshouses* on the Bath Road. The heath known as *Maidenhead Thicket*, S of the Bath Road, was a notorious haunt of highwaymen, and it is also the site of **Robin Hood's Arbour**, an Iron Age earthwork. From the 1860s Maidenhead was one of the Thames's most fashionable resorts, much favoured by the Brigade of Guards, which had its own clubhouse on the river. In Edwardian days **Boulter's Lock**, the longest and deepest on the Thames, was thronged

with summer pleasure boats. The name comes from the long fisherman's line with numerous hooks known as a 'boulter'. Of the many fine hotels and restaurants in the vicinity no doubt the most famous was Skindles, whose fashionable reputation established in Edwardian times burgeoned in the inter-war years. It is now the *Val Bon*.

Mapledurham
A2

Oxon. Village off A4074, 4m NW of Reading

A charming and secluded village of mellow red-brick houses and cottages running down to the Thames and the great house. **St Margaret's Church** (much restored in the 1860s) contains monuments to Sir Richard and Lady Cecily Blount (1620s) and a magnificent brass to Sir Robert Bardolf (d. 1395). The *Vicarage* was built by Lord Augustus FitzClarence, son of King William IV and the actress Mrs Jordan, vicar here from 1829 to 1854. There are pretty Jacobean Almshouses and (in the grounds of Mapledurham House) a picturesque old **Watermill**, recently restored, where fresh-ground flour can be bought.

Mapledurham House A private residence, the home of Mr J. J. Eyston, a descendant of the Blount family which built the original house between the 1580s and the 1620s; there have been important subsequent rebuildings and modifications. The stately exterior of patterned red brick is the result of late 18th-c. work; the alterations were completed in the 1830s. In the *Entrance Hall* is a collection of carved animal heads from the 17th and 18th c. The *Great Staircase* dates from the original house, and there are splendid 17th-c. plaster ceilings and friezes, as well as many excellent paintings. The family *Chapel* is in 1780s Gothick style. The poet Alexander Pope (d. 1744) was a close friend of the Blounts and a frequent visitor. It is said that the aspect of the house from across the Thames inspired Kenneth Grahame's description of Toad Hall. For today's visitors there are picnic places in the beautiful *Grounds*, which reach to the riverside.

Marlow
B2/C2

Bucks. Pop 14,132. 12m NW of Windsor (A404/A4155/B482). Event: Marlow Regatta (last week in Jun). EC Wed

This beautiful little resort town, with its famous suspension bridge over the Thames, is the improbable birthplace of the most famous monster in the world fiction, for it was while living here in 1818-19 that Mary Shelley wrote *Frankenstein*.

Mentioned in the Domesday Book (1086) as one of the manors of William the Conqueror's Queen Maud, Marlow has a long if uneventful history. In 1628 the town's MP Sir Miles Hobart made a name for himself when he locked the door of the Commons against the royal messenger of Charles I, being imprisoned in the Tower of London for his pains. In 1646 a stone monument to Hobart, now in the porch of Marlow's parish church, was erected by Parliament out of public funds – believed to be the first example of a public memorial. The town's principal industry was lace-making, but the old wharf did a large business as a river port for barges to London carrying wood brought down from High Wycombe, as well as flour, paper and brassware produced by numerous nearby watermills. Marlow's own historic mill was destroyed by fire in the 1960s. In 1802 the 12th-c. parish church was demolished due to its unsafe foundations, and its monumental brasses sold for scrap. In 1831 the old wooden bridge was replaced by the famous *Suspension Bridge* designed by the engineer Tierney Clarke; he was also the designer of the bridge over the Danube between Buda and Pest in Hungary, destroyed by the retreating German army in World War II.

The Marlow Regatta, now held in the last week of June and considered the dress rehearsal for the Henley Royal Regatta, has been an annual event since the 1870s. It comprises 15 events – five for eights, five for fours and five for pairs – and attracts an international entry. Special events during the regatta are a fair and fireworks display.

Tour Whether you approach Marlow from the S, across the bridge, or from the N, park if you can on-street in the Causeway down by the river, near the parish church of All Saints and the War Memorial. Nearby is the charming little *monument* to the theatrical impresario Charles Frohman (who regularly vacationed in Marlow and went down in the sinking of the *Lusitania* in May 1915) and the attractive *George and Dragon Hotel*, with its wall painting of Edwardian Marlow in the Regatta bar. The **Church of All Saints** (1835-70) with its 170-ft spire, provides the focus of a beautiful river frontage, best seen from the bridge. On the other side of the river stands the handsome *Compleat Angler Hotel*.

After enjoying the view from the bridge, proceed to **High Street** with its attractive old buildings. As you walk up, notice on the W side the *Little Stone House* (16th-c.), and porticoed Georgian *Brewery House*, and next to it, the *White House* (now a shop) with its double frontage of three-storey bay windows. Opposite, on the E side of High Street, is the 16th-c. *Chequers Inn*, picturesque and sturdy with its ship-timber frames. A few doors up a stately five-bayed red-brick Georgian mansion, with pillared porch, houses the *Post Office*. Near the top of High Street (E side), notice the distinguished gabled red-brick building, now boarded up, with behind it a secluded park-like garden of *New Court*. At the end of High Street stands an obelisk *milestone* on a little traffic island; behind this is *The Crown Inn* (built 1807), formerly the Market House, with the wooden lantern of the old Market Hall above it.

Turn left along *West Street* for pretty 16th- and 17th-c. frontages, one with a dragon gable ornament, and *The Coach and Horses Inn*, half-timbered and low gabled. Continuing down West Street you come to the double-bayed frontage of *Remnantz*; almost opposite stands the *Sir William Borlase School*, with, next to it, the house where the poet Shelley and his sister

Mary lived from March 1817 to February 1818. While she wrote *Frankenstein* he wrote *The Revolt of Islam*. At this time Thomas Love Peacock had a house in West Street, writing *Nightmare Abbey* there, while a century later T.S. Eliot lived for a time at No 31 West Street, the Old Post Office House.

Returning to High Street, retrace your steps towards the Causeway, but first turn left at Station Road for the handsome frontage of *Marlow Place* (early 18th-c.). A recent conversion has removed the staircase which once swept up to the entrance at first-floor level, set beneath a pediment surmounting the central three bays of the house and 'supported' on brick pilasters. Across the road is the *Old Parsonage* with interesting 14th-c. work – probably the oldest building surviving in Marlow. The nearby Catholic *Church of St Peter* contains a relic, supposed to be the hand of St James the Apostle, which up to the Reformation was kept in Reading Abbey.

If you leave Marlow along the Henley Road (continuation of West Street), look out for the 16th-c. *Hare and Hounds Inn*.

Medmenham
B2

Bucks. Village off A4155, 3m SW of Marlow

The chief landmark in this prosperous dormitory village is the 14th-c. pub, *The Dog and Badger*. Opposite to it stands **St Peter's Church**, Norman in origin with 15th-c. tower and timbered chancel, but heavily restored in the 19th and 20th c.; nearby stands the timber-framed *Manor House* among groves of beech and yew, and on the hillside above the house and barns of the 17th-c. *Lodge Farm* (NT). *Ferry Lane*, with its old cottages of flint, brick and timber-frame structure runs down to the old ferry crossing and the riverside site of Medmenham Abbey. The 12th-c. Cistercian abbey was plundered of its stone after the Dissolution of the Monasteries. The late Elizabethan house built here received 18th-c. 'Gothick' modifications under

Sir Francis Dashwood, who used it as a venue for the notorious Hell Fire Club (see **Wycombe*) and, it is said, supplemented it with erotic statues and an entrance door in the shape of a vagina. The present house, closed to the public, is the result of a 'clean-up' Victorian restoration, though some picturesque Gothick ruins do survive. It is advisable to park near the main road and walk down Ferry Lane.

Mill End see *Hambleden*

Molesey
D4

Surrey. Town on B369/B3379 (A3050), 4m E of Walton-on-Thames. Event: Molesey Amateur Regatta (2nd week in Apr, end Aug)

A pleasant stretch of towpath along a riverbank lined with houseboats runs from Molesey Lock to the cricket ground at Hurst Park. The East Molesey Cricket Club can boast a historic lineage: a notice board in its grounds records a match played in June 1735 between a Surrey XI selected by Frederick, Prince of Wales and a London XI – Surrey lost. There has been an unbroken tradition of cricket on this meadow ever since.

Hampton Court Bridge links the town to **Hampton Court Palace*. Near the bridge, on the Hampton Court side, is a splendid inn, *The Mitre*. Bridge Road, with its antique shops, runs S.

The Regatta, organised by the Molesey Boat Club, ranks with that at Marlow as second only to Henley's.

Old Windsor
C3

Berks. Village on A308, 2½m SE of Windsor. EC Wed

Lying between the Thames and the E edge of Windsor Great Park, this humble village was, at the time of Domesday Book in 1086, the third largest place in Berkshire. Excavation has revealed archaeological evidence of the Anglo-Saxon settlement, and indications of a royal palace ante-dating the Norman castle at Windsor by a century or so. At the turn of the 11th and 12th c. both William Rufus and Henry I held their courts here, but hereafter the place declined as a new town grew up at the foot of the great castle up-river. *St Peter's Church* by the river with its towers and shingled broach spire dates from the 14th c. It was restored in 1863-4 by Sir George Gilbert Scott.

Pangbourne
Berks. Town on A329 (A340, B471), 18m SW of Henley-on-Thames. EC Thur

A2

Described a hundred years ago as 'a pretty riverside village where the Thames seems especially fond of disporting itself, where it loiters in the great depths of the pools and creeps slyly under the banks', Pangbourne is still one of the most delightful spots in the Thames Valley. Sometime in the 1880s Jerome K. Jerome's *The Three Men in a Boat* and Montmorency the Dog visited *The Swan Hotel* down by the river, and it was to Pangbourne that the artist E.H. Shepard came to research the illustrations for Kenneth Grahame's *The Wind in the Willows* (published 1908). No doubt the amiable ghosts of Ratty and Mole still haunt the river banks hereabouts. The pool beneath the lock is a famed beauty spot, graced with a delightful view of the church rising behind the trees.

A sign at the N end of the main street commemorates Grahame, and also the 9th-c. King Beorhtwulf of Mercia who granted the Anglo-Saxon settlement here its borough charter. Since 1917 Pangbourne has been the home of the *Nautical College*.

Penn
Bucks. Village on B474, 3m NW of Beaconsfield

C1

The Penn family owned the manor here from the 13th c. to the 1730s, when it passed to the Curzons of Kedleston (William Penn belonged to a distant branch of the manorial family). With the neighbouring *Tylers Green* the village was the centre for tile making from the nearby clay beds, the tileries supplying baked tiles all over SE England, notably for the medieval palace of Westminster, for Hampton Court and for Windsor.

Once described by Sir John Betjeman as 'the Chelsea of the Chilterns', Penn lies along a high ridge with sloping beech woods and superb views, especially from the tower of **Holy Trinity Church**. Set among old yews and lime trees, the church was much restored in the 13th c. and a number of consecration crosses painted in roundels on the walls record the completion of the work. There are 17th-c. brasses to the Penn family in the S aisle, some fine hatchments, old box pews and a superb roof of black carved timbers from the 1380s. Over the chancel arch is a fine 14th-15th-c. painting of the Last Judgement on oak boards – a rare English example of panel painting. The beautiful and peaceful annexe to the churchyard was designed by Sir Edward Maufe in the late 1970s. Near the church is the charming old *Crown Inn* and S of the village stands *The Knoll*, a late 17th-c. mansion where Princess (later Queen) Anne lived during the reign of William III; her royal arms are in the church.

Radnage
Bucks. Village between A40 and A4010, 5m NW of High Wycombe

B1

A difficult place to find even when you get there. The winding lanes between the hamlets of Town End, Bennett End and The City (the largest!) are lined with bungalows and cottages. Do not miss *The Three Horseshoes* (1745) at Bennett End, an isolated but comfortable old pub complete with chimneys, gables, Georgian brick and car park, just up the hill from the little village green. The early 13th-c. **Church of St Mary's** at Town End, with its 15th-c. porch, is graced by an attractive central tower; the font is probably Saxon from an earlier church, having been unearthed in a neighbouring field.

Reading
Berks. Pop: 132,000. 17m W of Windsor (A4/A33/A327/A329/A4074/A4155). Events: Reading Arts Festival (May-Jun); Reading Amateur Regatta (Jun). MD Sat. Inf: Tel (0734) 592388/55911

A3

Reading is hardly picturesque in tourist terms, but as a centre of light industry and as a modern university town it is a place of some importance.

The **Museum and Art Gallery** is well known for its Roman archaeology collection and an interesting replica of the Bayeux Tapestry, while Reading University's **Museum of English Rural Life** at Whiteknights Park is a treasure-house of the implements and artefacts of an earlier age and has, besides, more than 300,000 photographs. The University's other museums are the **Ure Museum of Greek Archaeology**, showing pottery, and the **Cole Museum of Zoology**, which is a teaching museum.

The town, at the confluence of the Thames and River Kennet, arose from ancient settlements along the gravel terraces which were here some 30ft above the flood level of the Thames. There are traces of Roman villas in the vicinity, and the Roman city of Silchester once stood about 8m away. The Anglo-Saxon village here was overrun by Danish invaders in 871, and the place was razed by later Danish raiders in the early 11th c. In 1121 Henry I founded an Abbey here, later consecrated (1164) by Archbishop Thomas à Beckett in the presence of Henry II. For the rest of the Middle Ages it was one of England's greatest monastic foundations, and Parliament was convened here more than once. At this time the town was an important centre of the English cloth industry.

Reading's most famous citizens are: John Blagrave (d. 1611) a mathematician and astronomer of genius who made essential contributions to the science of navigation, and whose benefactions to the town included an annual prize for serving maids (the charity still exists though devoted to other objects); and William Laud (1573-1645), the controversial Archbishop of Canterbury under King Charles I, born near present Laud Place and executed for treason by Parliament. He also left generous endowments to the town, and helped win its royal charter from the king in 1638.

Reading suffered for its Royalist sympathies during the Civil War, but found renewed prosperity during the 18th c. exporting malt and corn downriver to London and becoming a noted centre for sail cloth manufacturing. Early in the 1800s the completion of the Kennet and Avon Canel brought new commerce to the town and the establishment of Sutton's Seeds and the Huntley and Palmer Biscuit factory meant further prosperity. In the 1880s, with a population approaching 90,000, Reading saw the foundation of an adult education college. Handsomely endowed by the Palmer family and Lady Wantage among others, the institute flourished and in the 1920s received its royal charter as the University of Reading.

In its long history, Reading has the melancholy distinction of being the place where the persecuted Oscar Wilde served his prison sentence from May 1895 to May 1897. It was here that he wrote his deeply moving testament *De Profundis* while his *Ballad of Reading Gaol* records the last miserable days of a murderer hanged there in July 1896.

Reading Abbey was commandeered by Henry VIII at the Dissolution of the Monasteries after the last Abbot had been hung, drawn and quartered before the gates on a trumped-up charge of treason. Henry took over the immense premises as a royal residence; today the ruins are few and scattered. They lie beside Forbury Road leading from the Station (an attractive Italianate building of the 1840s). Most conspicuous are the 12th-c. *Inner Gateway* by Abbots Walk, and the late 13th-c. *Inner Gatehouse*, much restored in the 1860s, which now serves as a museum. Some of the beautifully carved capitals from the pillars of the medieval abbey are to be seen in Reading Museum.

Other old churches include the 13th- and 14th-c. *Greyfriars*, at the junction of Friar Street and Greyfriars Road, with much 19th-c. work; the 12th-15th-c. *St Laurence's* on the Forbury Road, with some interesting medieval brasses and a handsome allegorical monument to John Blagrave; and for those interested in Victorian architecture, *Christ Church* in Christchurch Road (1860s), the most noteworthy of the numerous 19th-c. churches in the town. Perhaps the finest building in Reading is the majestic 1830s *Royal Berkshire Hospital* on the London Road, with its giant columned portico.

Rotherfield Greys   B2
Oxon. Village off B481, 3m W of Henley-on-Thames. Event: Village Festival, Greys Court (Jun)

Seat of the de Grey family from 1066 to the 1480s, the village stands in rich pasture-land (Anglo-Saxon *hryther*, 'cattle'). The **Church of St Nicholas** was largely re-built in 1865 but contains a superb brass to Lord Robert de Grey (d. 1387) in full armour, and the Knollys family chapel built in 1605 on the death of his wife by Lord William Knollys (possibly Shakespeare's model for Malvolio), Lord of the Manor. Here an impressive canopied monument of gilded marble and alabaster commemorates the founder and his wife and parents, Sir Francis and Lady Knollys (cousin to Elizabeth I).

The great country house, **Greys Court** (NT), on the edge of the village, was given to the National Trust in 1969 by Sir Felix Brunner. The *Great Tower* and three other towers survive from the medieval mansion. The present house of red brick, banded with flint, was built in the 16th c. by the Knollys family, Lords of the Manor from 1518 to 1708. In 1724 the manor passed to the Stapledon family, whose additions included the magnificent rococo plasterwork in the *N Drawing Room*. In the *Grounds* are three interesting buildings: the *Bachelor's Hall* (with its Latin inscription, 'There is nothing better than the celibate life'); to the E of it a beautiful old tulip tree and a weeping ash; the 17th-c. Cromwellian *Stables*, with the *Carlisle Collection* of miniature furnished rooms; and the early Tudor *Wheelhouse*, containing a massive donkey wheel winch.

From the tollgate near the house a good walk follows public footpaths and farm tracks, returning *via The Maltster's Arms* (see *Walk 5*, p.19).

Runnymede Meadows (NT)   C3
Surrey. On the Thames, 4m down-river from Windsor

It was here in June 1215 that King John gave his assent to Magna Carta, in the presence of his bishops and barons whose liberties it was designed to assure. At the W end of the meadows two islands in the Thames are popular picnic sites. The larger, called *Magna Carta Island* is, according to tradition, the site where the great charter was given the royal approval, though the actual document gives the place as 'in the meadow which is called Runnymede between Windsor and Staines.' The *Magna Carta Memorial* at the foot of *Cooper's Hill*, designed by Sir Edward Maufe, was presented by the American Bar Association and unveiled in 1957. Nearby lie some 3 acres of fields and woodlands which constitute the *John F. Kennedy Memorial*, made over in perpetuity to the people of the USA by Queen Elizabeth II in 1965. Atop Cooper's Hill stands the *Runnymede Memorial* (also designed by Maufe) dedicated in 1953 to the memory of men of the Commonwealth air forces, lost in action during World War II. N of the meadows stands the *Ankerwyke Yew*, some 33ft in circumference and supposed to have been a sapling in the days of King John.

Slough   C2
Berks. Pop 87,005. 2m N of Windsor (M4/A4/A355/A412). EC Wed MD Tue

The sprawl of housing and light industry – based on the 600-acre Slough Trading Estate – that makes up modern Slough offers, in all truth, little of interest to the tourist. Yet the place has historical associations of unexpected interest, and the village enclaves of **Upton*, **Stoke Poges* and **Langley Marish* on the N and E outskirts of the town are delightful.

For centuries part of the parish of Upton-cum-Chalvey, Slough derived its unprepossessing name from the low-lying marshy land along the Chalvey Brook, formerly a great centre for market gardening. It was here, from the 1830s, that the Cox's Orange Pippin made its commercial debut and the Sinkins Pink, among other flower varieties (cultivars), was developed. **Salt Hill**, an ancient tumulus in the centre of the town, was from about 1500 to the mid-19th c. the site of the annual 'ad Montem' ceremonial 'jolly' for the boys of Eton. Processing in costume to the little hill they were wont to extort 'contributions' from travellers and the citizenry, offering in exchange lumps of salt. In the 18th c. this strange activity attracted visitors from London society, and later the young Queen Victoria enjoyed attending. However, the high-minded Dr Hawtrey, Eton's famous headmaster in the mid-1800s, put a stop to the proceedings, which he considered lawless and rowdy (among other things it was said that the arrival of the railway at Slough had opened the 'ad Montem' to pickpockets and petty criminals from the capital).

The waters of the Chalvey Brook, which were supposed to have medicinal properties, brought other visitors to Slough. Queen Anne took the waters here, while King George III had the drinking water for Windsor Castle carried from the Chalvey. During the 18th c., too, the place became a major staging post for the new mail coach service, the town's many hostelries having stabling for more than 1000 horses. Then in the 1780s Sir William Herschel, the town's most famous resident, took a house near the crossroads. The discoverer of the planet Uranus (1781), he erected a massive telescope (40ft x 5ft in diameter) in his new home and made Slough, in the opinion of a visiting French scientist ' . . . the place in the world where most discoveries have been made, a village whose name shall never perish.' The great astronomer was buried at *Upton church, but in 1960 Slough signalled its respect for his memory by permitting the destruction of the Herschel family home, known for generations as Observatory House.

In the 1830s Slough was the focus of a famous legal battle between Isambard Kingdom Brunel (for the Great West-

ern Railway) and Eton College. Fearing the effect of mass travel on their peaceful neighbouring village and also the temptations it would place in the way of their boys, the College authorities fought to stop the building of a station at Slough. In 1838 they finally admitted defeat, and four years later Queen Victoria set royal approval on the railway age by entraining at Slough for her first rail journey. In 1845 Slough station wrote a new page in the annals of technology when the murderer John Tawell was arrested on arrival at the GWR's London terminus as the result of his description being telegraphed down the line – the first criminal to be caught with the aid of the electric telegraph. The coming of the railway brought the first age of industrialization to Slough, and by the late 19th c. it was considered ' . . . the home of dust and noise, steam, whistle and coal odours.' Now part of the growing national transport network, Slough's businessmen took advantage of the expanding domestic market. James Elliman, a local draper, built a vast fortune from his patent medicine Elliman's Embrocation (now part of the Horlicks Group with its factory at Slough). His family proved generous benefactors to the town.

The one building of historic interest in Slough is the 17th-18th-c. *Baylis House*, off Stoke Poges Lane to the N. Built for a Dean of Windsor, it passed to the Godolphin family of Eton early in the 1700s, and the dolphins of their coat-of-arms can be seen on the wrought-iron gates. It was they who built the handsome stable block with its classical colonnade and lantern roof.

Sonning　　　　　　　　　　　　　　　　　　　B2
Berks. Village on B478 (A4), on NE outskirts of Reading

Perhaps the most beautiful village on the lower Thames, this is a place of stately 17th-and 18th-c. houses, handsome old inns such as *The Bull*, and a white weather-boarded *Mill* along the willow-lined banks of the river. Once the site of a palace of the bishops of

Salisbury, part of which still survives in the S wall of the churchyard, Sonning offers many fine brasses and monuments in its *Church*. Apart from a fine 15th-c. tower, the building itself is heavily restored with both 19th-and 20th-c. work. The lovely mellow brick *bridge* dates from the 18th c.

Staines
D3

Surrey. Pop 56,380. 6m SE of Windsor (A30/A308). Events: Staines Amateur Regatta (Jul); Staines Boat Regatta (late Aug). EC Thur MD Wed, Sat

The sprawling modern town has few surviving indications of its long history. There seems to have been a Roman bridge here; the place is mentioned in Magna Carta (1215) and the '*London Stone*', in what is now the Ashby Recreation Ground, was erected in 1285. The stone marked the limit of the jurisdiction of the City of London. Near to the town are the extensive *Staines Reservoirs* which supply much of London's water. About 1m upstream is *Bell Weir Lock*, which offers good fly fishing, and the meadows of Runnymede.

On the A320 road to Chertsey lies **Thorpe Park** with its water gardens, bird sanctuary, nature trail and farm. Among the many other attractions of this family pleasure park, the Schneider Trophy plane and *Exhibition* of aircraft of World War I are of special historic interest; the Treasure Island and Riverboat Restaurant are also recommended.

Stoke Poges
C2

Bucks. Village on B416, on N outskirts of Slough

It was in the churchyard here that Thomas Gray was inspired with the idea for his 'Elegy in a Country Churchyard' in the 1740s. **St Giles** is approached through a lych-gate, and the yews and cypresses of its churchyard still conjure the mood of the great poem. You enter through a handsome timber porch to a 12th-c. nave with a massive 14th-c. timber roof. The N tower, S aisle and chancel are also 12th-c. Norman work; the N aisle is later, and the *Hastings Chapel* 16th-c.

There are medieval brasses, monuments to the 18th-c. Penn family who bought the manor in the 18th c. and a simple grave slab to Thomas Gray E of the Hastings Chapel. An unusual feature, in a stained-glass window, is the depiction of a medieval 'bicycle'. The monumental stone *sarcophagus* in the field outside the church gate was put up to designs by James Wyatt in 1799. Close to the church lies the peaceful *Garden of Remembrance* with a lake, fountain and rose garden.

The first *Manor House* was built for Robert de Pogies in the 12th c. The present Elizabethan building behind the church is part of the house built by Sir Edward Coke, Chief Justice and Attorney General to Queen Elizabeth I, whom he entertained here, and James I. He prosecuted in the trial of Sir Walter Raleigh, but lost royal favour in 1616 and was later to be a champion of parliament.

In the 18th c. the manor was bought by Thomas Penn (d. 1775) who built *Stoke Park*. Its white stucco and Doric porticoes, designed by Robert Nasmyth and James Wyatt, now provide a lordly setting for the clubhouse of the local golf club. Both Capability Brown and Humphry Repton worked on the landscaping of the grounds, and the former Rectory was demolished to make way for **Gray's Monument** (NT), designed as a 'feature' to be seen from the house.

Thomas Gray (1716-71) has many associations with Buckinghamshire, having spent part of his boyhood at Burnham and been educated at Eton. From 1742 to 1753, when not in residence at Cambridge, he lived with his mother and aunt in West End Cottage, ¾m N of the church and now part of *Stoke Court*. Here he wrote his 'Ode on a Distant Prospect of Eton College' and began the 'Elegy'. It took him more than eight years in the writing, and visits to the Church of St Lawrence at nearby **Upton* may well have provided some of the inspiration for the work. Some people hold that it was the main inspiration.

At *Stoke Green*, to the SE of Stoke Poges, lies *Stoke Place*, a 17th-18th-c. mansion of brick in grounds landscaped by Capability Brown. To the E of Stoke Poges, *Black Park* and *Langley Park*, noted for its rhododendron gardens, offer beautiful walks.

Stonor Park   B1
Oxon. Historic house on B480, 5m N of Henley.
Event: Chiltern Crafts Show (Aug)

The home of Lord and Lady Camoys and of their family, the Stonors, since Anglo-Saxon times, the great house on its wooded hillside commands magnificent views. The 13th-c. core of the house has some of the oldest domestic architecture in England but, thanks to successive modifications, the great mansion now presents a handsome redbrick Georgian façade, centred by a gabled porch with the original medieval doorway and 18th-c. Gothick windows. The 'Gothick' theme was continued in some of the interiors and the house is rich in stained-glass windows, some interesting furniture (notice the bedroom suite in sea-shell forms), paintings, sculptures and tapestries. The Stonors remained true to their Catholic faith during the Reformation; the priest St Edmund Campion found refuge here in 1581. The medieval *Chapel* has been in use for Mass continuously for over 800 years.

From the hillside behind the house is a good view of the surrounding *Deer Park* and woodlands.

Sunbury   D4
Surrey. Town on M3/A244/A308/B375, 12m SE of Windsor. EC Thur. Inf: Tel (76) 51499

A charming and popular riverside town, with good coarse fishing in the weir and sluices above Sunbury Lock. Built in 1925 to replace a wooden one dating from the 1810s, the lock lies in an island which can be reached by ferry from the town – a foot-bridge gives access to the weirs. *St Mary's Church*, with its unusual cupola and lantern, overlooks the river; it was built in the 1750s and extended with porch and apse a century later. The *Kempton Park Racecourse* lies to the N.

Taplow   C2
Bucks. Village off A4, 2m E of Maidenhead

The 19th-c. Norman-style *Mansion* is the home of Lord and Lady Desborough, while 2m N lies the great house of **Cliveden*. Charming old cottages and modern villas are set among the meadows, and wooded slopes give the place an air of refurbished opulence. The **Church**, rebuilt in the 20th c. in Gothic style, contains the old Norman font of the original church and a number of good brasses from the 15th and 16th c.

Turville   B1
Bucks. Village between B480 & B482, 6½m N of Henley-on-Thames

One of the most picturesque of the Chiltern villages, Turville lies in its dry hollow backed by a green cliff-like slope of turf on which stands the old *Smock Windmill*. **St Mary's Church**, with a squat 13th-c. tower, contains its original Norman font, and traces of the Norman structure can still be seen among the 13th-c. work and the 14th-c. timber roof. There are some interesting monuments, a pretty pillared wooden screen and a lunette window in the nave by John Piper.

A country walk along public footpaths through fields and woods leads to **Fingest*, 1½m E (see *Walk 4*, p.18).

Tylers Green see *Penn*

Upton   C3
Berks. Village on S outskirts of Slough

Despite its uninspiring neighbour, Slough, Upton retains its character and has quiet echoes of a peaceful past. Standing at a busy crossroads, the **Church of St Lawrence** is a fine example of a Norman parish church (the S aisle was added in the 1850s). Notice the rib-vaulting of its 12th-c. chancel, decorated in red, black and yellow and ziz-zag mouldings. Here lies buried Sir William Herschel (d. 1822) the great astronomer, whose house nearby, demolished in the 1960s, witnessed many of his discoveries. Screened from the church by trees lies *Upton Court*. The original house was built in the 15th c.

for the monks of Merton Abbey. During the 18th c. Upton Court was home of the Lascelles family, ancestors of Lord Harewood; in the 19th c. Joseph Paxton, designer of the Crystal Palace, laid out the grounds of the house for the Herschel family. *The Red Cow* at Upton is a comfortable inn dating back to the 17th c.

Waltham St Lawrence B2

Berks. Village on B3024, 9m W of Windsor

The fine old timber-framed *Bell Inn* here dates back, it is said, to the 14th c.; the brick and timber cottage next door is probably 15th-c. The Victorian-restored *Church of St Lawrence*, medieval in origin, has an interestingly early 17th-c. pulpit and a number of lovely monuments, notably the 1650s memorial to Katherine Thomas.

Walton-on-Thames D4

Surrey. Town on A3050/A244, 18m SE of Windsor. Event: Walton Regatta (Jun). EC Wed. Inf: Tel (0932) 228844

Tradition has it that the Romans forded the Thames here in their campaign against the Celtic chief Cassivellaunus, and a hoard of Roman 3rd-4th-c. coins was discovered in the early 1900s. **St Mary's Church**, with traces of Anglo-Saxon work still to be seen in the structure of the N wall, has some fine medieval brasses and later monuments as well as a 'scolds' bridle'. As well as the regatta, punting and skiff races are held here in the summer.

West Wycombe (NT) C1

Bucks. Village on A40, 1m W of High Wycombe

For miles around, the remarkable gilded globe atop the Church of St Lawrence, with the colonnades of its adjacent mausoleum, landmarks one of the most fascinating spots in the region. No doubt the main attractions are the notorious Hell Fire Caves and Wycombe Park, home of the Dashwood family, but do not miss the village – a uniquely preserved 18th-c. country township.

Approaching from High Wycombe you come first to *The Pedestal*, a mile post erected in 1752 to commemorate

the completion of a new road by Sir Francis Dashwood. It indicates the distances to 'The City' (London), the 'County Town' (Aylesbury) and to the 'University', i.e. Oxford, and is a fitting introduction to the lordly eccentricities of the noble landlord. Next on the right is the 15th-c. *Church Loft* with its overhanging upper storey and 17th-c. bell turret; then the 18th c. takes over. *The Swan, The Plough* and *The George and Dragon Inns* recall a bygone age when stage coaches jostled with drovers watering their cattle in the stream running down the High Street. By the 1920s, however, the place had become derelict. In 1929 it was bought by the Royal Society of Arts who, after restoration, handed the village over to the National Trust in 1934. At the W end of the village are a *Garden Centre*, the gates of Wycombe Park, and, sharp right, the little road leading up to the Hell Fire Caves. All have car parks. The church, mausoleum and caves do not belong to the Trust.

West Wycombe Park (NT) This is the proper place to begin an account of West Wycombe, since much of the village and its monuments were built by the Dashwoods. The family made its fortune in the 17th c. from trade with the Turkish Ottoman Empire and China, and bought the manor in 1698. The first Queen Anne house (1710s) provided the nucleus for the mansion created by Sir Francis Dashwood (1708-81). The place reflects his diverse interests and talents, based on wide travels in Europe including both Greece and Russia. He was a founder member of the Dilettante Society, important for pioneering publications on the ruins of ancient Greece; a Fellow of the Royal Society; a member of parliament for 20 years and joint postmaster general from 1765 until his death. That great American polymath and man of affairs Benjamin Franklin, a frequent guest at West Wycombe, described Sir Francis as a man of 'kind countenance . . . intelligent conversation who, having . . . seen all parts of Europe and kept the best company in the world, is himself the best existing.'

The magnificent *S front* of the house, with its two-storeyed colonnades, was completed to designs by the architect John Donowell in 1754; the columned W portico, the main entrance designed by Nicholas Revett, in 1771. Revett was also responsible for the charming classical Music Temple on its island in the lake, and for the stables and other structures. The pervading architectural style is late Palladian, but the building incorporated technically advanced features for the period such as underfloor hot-air heating. The interiors are comfortably elegant with many magnificent chimney pieces, fine marquetry in the *Music Room*, beautiful rococo ceiling paintings in the *Library* and much fine 18th-c. furniture. Robert Adam was among the designers.

The *Park*, a model of 18th-c. English landscape gardening, was begun in the mid-1730s. The lake, formed by damming the River Wye, was the scene of mock battles between a fleet of four little ships; the serpentine streams and paths gave vistas closed by follies and classical temples and, more practically, a sawmill house: this was surmounted by a 6ft-high lead statue of William Penn, founder of Pennsylvania, presented in 1804 to the Pennsylvania hospital in Philadelphia, where it still stands. Humphry Repton was commissioned in the 1790s to 'tidy up' the elaborate layout of the park.

The Hell Fire Caves Lying between the church on the hill and the village, the caves derive their name from the Hell Fire Club, otherwise known as the Knights of St Francis of Wycombe, formed by Dashwood and his friends in 1746. Their badge included a travesty of a bishop's mitre, their weekend chapters held at *Medmenham Abbey comprised rumoured orgies of drinking and mock religious rites in which girls were dressed as nuns, and their motto was *Fay ce que voudras*, 'Do as you will'. The Club transferred to the caves at West Wycombe in the early 1760s,

and visitors today can walk the labyrinthine passages to the accompaniment of a taped commentary among life-like figures of ghostly rakes in their 18th-c. finery and tableaux hinting at their activities. The caves were part of an old chalk quarry which was reopened in 1748 by order of Sir Francis to provide material for his new road to High Wycombe. The workings provided employment for about 100 men in a period of poor harvests and economic depression – and also a fine new subterranean home for the Hell Fire Club.

The **Church of St Lawrence** stands high above the village within the mounds of an Iron Age *hill fort* (c. 400 BC, the earliest settlement known in the area) and on the site of a medieval church which served the vanished village of Haveringdon. In the 16th c. the villagers of West Wycombe seem to have worshipped in the Church Loft, High Street. In the 1750s Sir Francis Dashwood rebuilt St Lawrence's, as much for his own amusement, one feels, as for the benefit of the village. The golden ball above the 80ft tower was modelled on that of the Customs Building in Venice (16th-c.) and is made of wood, covered with gold leaf on canvas. Some 20ft in diameter, it can seat eight people. Sir Francis and his friends, among them John 'Liberty' Wilkes the radical MP and Lord Sandwich, drank many a 'divine punch' there, singing bawdy songs, the small windows giving glimpses of the superb views below.

The church is opened on most afternoons during the summer and occasionally during the winter; the interior with its richly painted coffered ceiling, giant columns and marble pavements, reflects a classical inspiration. Below the church is the **Mausoleum Monument** built by Dashwood in 1765 with a bequest from his friend Bubb Doddington of the Hell Fire Club. It takes the form of a hexagon of arches and niches open to the sky, each side 70ft long and with three large ornamental urns at each corner. An urn containing the heart of Paul Whitehead, poet and steward of the notorious club, was solemnly installed in the mausoleum in 1774.

Church and mausoleum form part of the **Wycombe Farm and Forest Trail**, established by the Chiltern Society in 1973 (see *Walk 1*, p.18). On Chorley Road, ¼m from the A40, the **West Wycombe Motor Museum** is housed in 18th-c. timbered barns. Changing exhibitions show historic motor bikes and cars.

Weybridge D4
Surrey. Pop 51,270 (incl. Walton). 10m SE of Windsor (A317). Event: Weybridge Amateur Regatta (Spring Bank Hol). EC Wed

Set among pleasant hills, Weybridge is typical of the residential areas on the Thames now heavily built up. On the Walton road is *Oatlands Park*, formerly a royal domain. The estate was on the western extremity of Henry VIII's deer park, and in 1537 the king took it over and built a hunting lodge and palace here. The palace was demolished in the Civil War and later (1794) rebuilt by the 'Grand Old Duke of York'. After the death of the Duchess of York (1820) Oatlands was sold and became a hotel in the 1860s.

The neo-Gothic *Church* (1840s) retains monuments and brasses from its medieval predecessor. In Church Street, above the library, is the **Weybridge Museum**, with exhibits of local and natural history, and archaeology; there are also small displays from the Surrey Costume Collection. Between Weybridge and Byfleet (SW), the Brooklands Motor Racing Track witnessed many historic meetings between the wars. The **Brooklands Museum**, scheduled to open here in 1986, recalls those days. Aviation is represented as well as motor racing.

The Thames Punting Club holds its annual regatta on the reach between Weybridge and Chertsey Bridge. There is good fishing not only in the Thames hereabouts but also in the Rivers Wey and Mole and the Weybridge Navigation Channel, opened in 1653 and now under the care of the National Trust.

White Waltham B2
Berks. Village off B3024, 8m W of Windsor

There are two charming 15th-c. brasses in the floor of the chancel of **St Mary's Church**. The chancel is a beautiful example of 13th-c. architecture, but the church as a whole was much restored in the 19th c. Near the church is a splendid old aisled barn and the old village stocks and whipping post.

Windsor
Berks. Pop 30,500. 24m W of London (M4/A308/ A332/A355/). Events: Royal Windsor Horse Show (Home Park, May); Championship Dog Show (Home Park, Jul); Windsor Festival (Sep-Oct); National Carriage Driving Championships (Smith's Lawn, Sep). EC Wed MD Sat. Inf: Tel (95) 52010

Leaving the M4 motorway at Junction 6 you approach Windsor along the A332; at the roundabout near the town centre follow the signs for Datchet, and park in the car park in River Street. (If this is full, there is another convenient park on the Datchet road.)

The history of the town is an adjunct to that of the great castle which gave it birth. Thanks to the royal favour of Edward I, Windsor was one of the medieval England's parliamentary boroughs, returning two MPs from 1306. The wealth of the town has always depended on the court and the castle staff, and its position today as one of the most prosperous towns in southern England depends, of course, on its character as a major tourist centre. For all this, and despite the dominating attractions of the castle, the town itself has much that is attractive and interesting.

At the head of River Street runs Thames Street, with the *Theatre Royal* down to your left and attractive shopping arcades and winding courts giving off the road as it swings round under the massive curtain wall of the castle's outer precincts. Ahead you see the famous *statue* of Queen Victoria with the Guildhall in the distance; on your right, continuing along Thames Street towards the statue and the Castle Hill approach to the castle gate, you pass the road leading down to *Windsor and Eton Central Station*. Here you will find not only the *Tourist Information Centre*

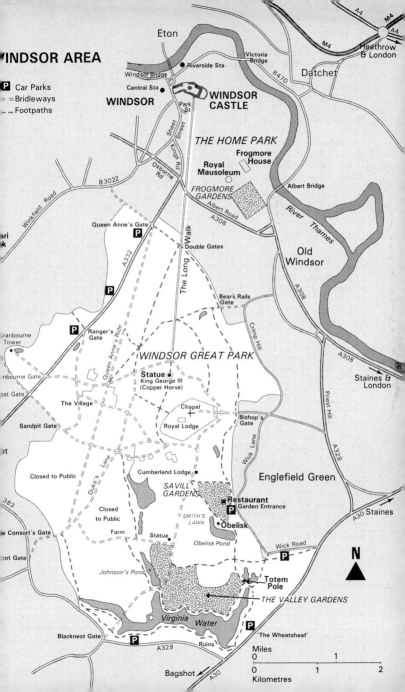

but the recently opened **Royalty & Empire** permanent exhibition of tableaux, representing with great realism the arrival of members of Europe's royalty come to congratulate Queen Victoria on the occasion of her Diamond Jubilee in 1897. Apart from numerous surprisingly life-like waxwork figures, the exhibit includes a full-scale reconstruction of coaches of the royal train and the locomotive that pulled it on this occasion. There is an audio-visual show, with moving tableaux, and a *Museum* housing treasures from the Guildhall. The admission charge is reasonable and the exhibition, which was mounted by the Madame Tussaud organization, is of outstanding interest.

Beyond the Queen's statue you come to the Guildhall, passing the fascinating old *Leaning Market House* on your left. The building of the **Guildhall** was completed in 1690 under the supervision of Sir Christopher Wren. A brick structure with stone dressings, it stands on arched bays supported on classical columns over an open ground floor. There are statues of Queen Anne (1707) on the N side and her husband Prince George of Denmark (1713) on the S side. Inside the open ground floor is a strange group of *columns*, apparently supporting the floor of the council chamber above, but in fact stopping short of it by an inch or two. When the hall was being built, so goes the story, the worthies of Windsor did not believe that the design was structurally safe and insisted on the extra pillars. Wren provided them, but had his little joke at the same time to indicate that whatever the clients thought, he and the designer knew what they were doing.

A little further on you come to Windsor's parish **Church of St John the Baptist** (1820s) with an interesting 17th-c. painting of The Last Supper and the *Windsor Brass Rubbing Centre*, where enthusiasts may rub their own impressions from replicas of some of the most famous monumental brasses of southern England. At the end of the High Street turn back down St Alban's

M4 & London

A332

WINDSOR — RELIEF — ROAD

CLEWER VILLAGE

Swimming Pool

STOVELL ROAD

A308

Windsor Racecourse

ART

B3024

CLARE

GOSLAR WAY

IMPERIAL ROAD

Household Cavalry M

B3173/B3022 Safari Park

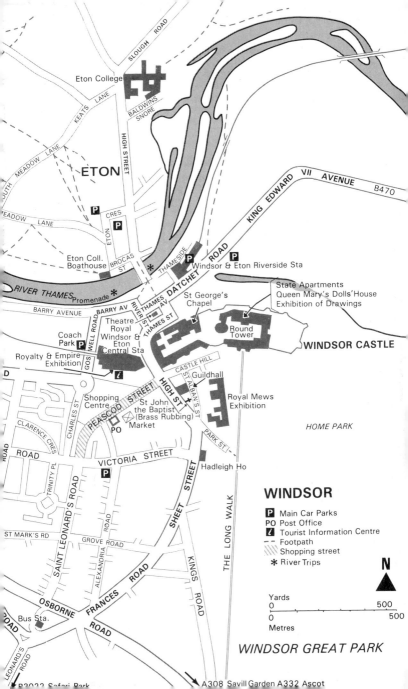

Street for the **Royal Mews Exhibition**. The star attraction is the Scottish State Coach, used for the wedding of Prince Charles and Princess Diana in July 1981; there is also a selection of the gifts presented to the Queen on the occasion of the Silver Jubilee of her reign in 1977. Here also the visitor can learn something of the elaborate business of maintaining the royal carriages and ceremonial horses. Another fascinating exhibition will be found at the **Household Cavalry Museum** in the Combermere Barracks (1960s) in St Leonard's Road in the S of the town. Its collection of militaria from the 17th c. to the present includes a magnificent collection of swords and uniforms.

Windsor Race Course, down by the river just beyond the village of Clewer, is well signposted for race meetings. These are held between January and November, there being no fewer than 10 meetings between early July and early September. Details may be had from the Secretary of the Course, Tel (95) 65234.

3½m SW of Windsor on the B3022 is **Windsor Safari Park**, where seven drive-through reserves, in a total area of 140 acres, give views of wild animals from all over the world in natural surroundings. Other attractions include a children's farmyard and amusement complex, picnic areas, a boating lake and *Safari Seaworld*, which besides keeping performing seals, dolphins, penguins and other examples of marine wildlife, boasts its own killer whale.

Windsor from the Castle

Index